THE CRAFT OF TATTING

other BELL & HYMAN Handbooks

Fabric Printing and Dyeing at Home
by Georgina Alexander

Creative Embroidery Collage
by Sadie Allen

Decorating with Stitches
by Lynette DeDeane and Margaret Johnson

Dyes from Natural Sources
by Anne Dyer

Canvas Work from the Start
by Anne Dyer and Valerie Duthoit

Modern Basketry from the Start
by Barbara Maynard

Pressed Plants as an Art
by Hilda Robinson

Mend Your Own China and Glass
by Susan Wells

Corn Dollies from the Start
by Emmie White

Your Machine for Embroidery
by Joy Clucas

Make Your Own Hats
by Jennifer Stuart

Rugmaking
by Joan Droop

Bobbin Lace Making
by Doreen Wright

Modern Upholstery
by Dorothy Cox

How to Make Dolls' Houses
by Audrey Johnson

How to Repair and Dress Old Dolls
by Audrey Johnson

Dressing Dolls
by Audrey Johnson

Furnishing Dolls' Houses
by Audrey Johnson

The Craft of Tatting

by Bessie M. Attenborough

Demonstrator and Teacher of Tatting to the
National Federation of Women's Institutes

Bell & Hyman : London

Published by
BELL & HYMAN LIMITED
Denmark House
37–39 Queen Elizabeth Street
London SE1 2QB

First published in 1972 by
G. BELL AND SONS LTD
Reprinted 1979

ISBN 0 7135 1704 2

*Printed and bound in Great Britain at
The Camelot Press Ltd, Southampton*

CONTENTS

page

Abbreviations   7

Introduction   8

EQUIPMENT for Tatting   11

TERMS used in Tatting   12

Method of working   13
  Making the stitches   13
  To make picots   16
  To make rings   16
  Picots made over a piece of card   17
  To join the rings   18
  The half ring   18
  The mock ring   18
  The chain   18
  Tatting with two threads   20
  Weaving in of threads   20
  Josephine knot   22
  Working an edging of rings directly on to a hem   22
  Mountings and Finishings   23

HANDKERCHIEFS   25
  Shuttle only   25
  Ball and shuttle   29
  Josephine knot   30

Edgings for Mats   34

Medallion inserted in a Tray Cloth   43

Trimmings for Children's Clothes   46

Cake Frill and Napkin Ring   50

		page
MATS		52
Luncheon Mats		52
Occasional Mats		56
Table Mats		76
COLLARS		79
LAMPSHADES		86
Edgings		86
Trimmings		88
Edgings for Towels		90
HANDBAGS		92
Linen Bag with Medallions		92
Summer handbag		94
Covered Buttons		96
Finger Plate for a Door		99
Drip Mats and Glass Mats		100
Lady's Choker		102
Framed Medallion		103
Recommended Books		104
Suppliers		104

ACKNOWLEDGMENTS

The author wishes to express her thanks to Mr A. G. Lacey who has taken all the photographs in the book; to Mr Charles Dovey for presenting her with many designs made by his late wife, Mrs Dorothy Dovey; to Messrs J. & P. Coats, for permission to use some of their designs; and to the publishers of the Penelope Needlecraft Publications for allowing her to use their designs, though they are now out of print.

ABBREVIATIONS

```
    * = repeat
    r = ring
   sr = small ring
   lr = large ring
   ds = double stitch
    p = picot
  smp = small picot
   lp = long picot
  sep = separated
   cl = close
   RW = reverse work
   sp = space
   ch = chain
  tog = together
  sjk = small josephine knot
  ljk = large josephine knot
```

Messrs Coats have kindly given permission for the following patterns to be reproduced from their Sewing Group Books:

Edging for Luncheon Mats (page 52): No. 469. Gay Place Mat or Occasional Mat (page 56): Book No. 813. Luncheon Mat in Two Colours (page 58): Book No. 813. Dressing Table Mat (page 76): Book No. 919.

INTRODUCTION

This book is intended to explain the age-old craft of Tatting as simply as possible, and to enable the beginner to learn and enjoy one of the most creative and, at the same time, one of the most relaxing of hobbies. Like many other crafts, tatting seems difficult at the first few attempts, but once mastered, it can become superlatively easy to do. Being light and easy to hold, simple to do, and with very little strain on the eyes, it can be a source of joy to many, and a great help and relaxation to the invalid.

Tatting in its modern form is lace making at its most exquisite. It has developed from the rudimentary looping and knotting of threads into circles and rings, as performed in Egypt in ancient times. The craft later appeared in China where it was widely practised, chiefly in the form of edgings. In the East the Orientals still retain the ancient designation of 'makouk' from the shape of the shuttles with which it is worked. It spread westward to Europe, where, in Italy it was called 'occhi' meaning eyes, from the shape of the rings; in France 'frivolité', denoting the fragile appearance of the work; and in Germany 'schiffchen-arbeit' or little boat work, from the shape of the shuttle.

The first recorded reference to Tatting in England is in a poem published by Sir Charles Sedley in 1707 and called 'The Royal Knotter', a compliment to Queen Mary's tatting habits. Dating from later in the century two famous pictures, one by Sir Joshua Reynolds of the Countess of Albemarle and now in the National Gallery, the other by Allan Ramsay of the Countess Temple, show ladies holding shuttles.

The name Tatting is derived apparently from the word 'tatters' denoting the fragile, disjointed nature of the work at its first introduction, the little rings all being made separately and then sewn on to the material with needle and thread, to form patterns.

It seems to have suffered a decline later on, but a revival began towards the middle of the nineteenth century, due to the influence of Mlle Riego who wrote a number of books on the subject and is really the founder of modern techniques, especially that of joining picots with the shuttle, and the introduction of the true chain on which all modern tatting design depends.

In the early years of this century, Queen Marie of Roumania and Lady Hoare did a great deal to improve the techniques and designs which could be used.

Tatting was taken to America by the Pilgrims and was used by the women to beautify their homes. It has remained very popular there since those days. It has also spread to Australia and New Zealand where it has steadily increased in popularity.

Uses for Tatting

Tatting was used originally for trimmings for furnishings, thick cotton being chiefly employed. With the advent of modern threads, in cottons and silks, designs of intricate beauty and delicate charm have evolved. The adaptations and uses of the craft are endless. Here are some of them:

Fashion Accessories

Collars or edgings for collars. Yokes for dresses and tops of evening dresses. Edgings, insertions and motifs for children's clothes. Chokers made entirely of tatting and mounted on velvet or comprised of a motif in the centre of a band of velvet. Gloves can either be made entirely of tatting or decorated with motifs to give them added charm.

Ladies' evening bags, handbags, powder compact cases, or spectacle cases, can be adorned with tatting. A bride's coronet and trimming for her dress and veil will make for originality and elegance. Other fashion articles designed and completed by the author at various times have been: covering for buttons, sprays of stylised flowers which can be pinned to a dress or coat, small motifs set into a brooch and belts trimmed with motifs.

Hats trimmed with tatted motifs take on the appearance of model hats, while an ordinary plain handkerchief is converted to a thing of beauty by the addition of a narrow edging of tatting.

As fashions change, so the designs in tatting can be modified and altered so that it is never out-dated and is always given that 'in fashion' look.

Furnishing and Household Uses

The applications of Tatting to household accoutrements are equally many and varied and adaptations can always be made to suit the period effect required.

Edgings and insertions for such things as guest towels, pillow cases or even sheets will give a distinction and unique charm to these articles. Edgings for mats of all descriptions give an added beauty to something quite ordinary, as will be seen from some of the examples shown later in this book.

Table mats, place mats and tray cloths made completely in tatting will enhance the beauty of the china, glass and cutlery placed thereon. Drip mats and glass mats, while adding elegance provide protection to polished surfaces.

Collage can be made from motifs of varying size, using a variety of threads, such as pure silk, embroidery cotton, fine string, Sylko, using several strands of different colours, round metallic threads, in short, anything you can find in the workbasket that will wind upon a shuttle, to give a variety of texture. The design of these must be left to the imagination and skill of the individual worker.

Miniatures made from medallions, worked in beautiful colours, mounted on velvet and set in small frames, can be very appealing. Bell pulls, wall panels and finger plates for doors also offer possibilities for the modern tatter. Chair backs are another form of furnishing to which tatting is peculiarly adapted, since many and varied designs can be used.

Other Uses

Lady Hoare and Queen Marie of Roumania used the craft to enhance and beautify church vestments and some of these were made even more startlingly beautiful by the addition of precious stones, which somehow were 'tatted in'.

The author herself has made a complete set of Church Linen, using tatting to edge the linen and medallions to decorate all the pieces.

Readers can no doubt think of many other uses to which Tatting might be put.

Equipment for Tatting

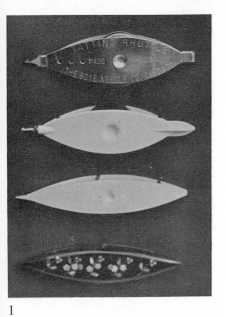

1   THE SHUTTLE

1. *The American Shuttle*
This shuttle is slim and easy to use, is made of chrome or stainless steel, has a detachable bobbin around which the cotton is wound. It also has a hook attached, with which to draw a thread through a picot.

2. *The English Shuttle*
New Aero Shuttle made by Abel Morrell of Redditch. This is made of plastic with steel hook attached at the end for pulling through a thread. Separate bobbin for cotton which only unwinds when pulled. It is light and easy to use and has a spare bobbin. Projection on end of shuttle on which to put the bobbin for winding.

3. *The Aluminium Shuttle*
This shuttle made by Aero is now out of production, but many people still use it. It does not have a spare bobbin, but a bar in the centre on which to wind the thread.

4. *The Victorian Shuttle*
A beautiful hand-made shuttle, probably of tortoiseshell and inlaid with mother-of-pearl. This also has a bar in the centre around which

11

the thread is wound. A crochet hook must be used to pull the thread through a picot.

SCISSORS
These must be small and sharp at the tips.

THREADS
These must be tightly twisted, and smooth and even in texture in order to give a fine appearance to the work. Immediately we think of Coats' crochet cottons, and these come in a variety of colours and thicknesses. The thickness of the cotton should always match the weight of the material. Other cottons and silks can be used as in the picture on the title page. Sylko can be used for the delicate edgings on lawn handkerchiefs and the one shown in the picture on page 35 is worked directly on to the handkerchief.

TERMS USED IN TATTING

DS DOUBLE STITCH
This is comprised of two halves of a knot, one made under the thread and one over the thread. When these are worked together they form the double stitch used throughout tatting.

R RING
This is made entirely of double stitches, worked on the shuttle thread only, and drawn tightly together, by the shuttle thread, to form a ring.

CH CHAIN
A chain is a bar of double stitches, worked with both shuttle and ball thread.

P PICOT
Picots are the small loops on the outside of the rings and chains, which make the work more attractive, and which are used to join the rings and chains together.

JK JOSEPHINE KNOT
This is made of a number of single stitches, namely the first or second half of the double stitch, and pulled up to make a small knot or ring.

RW REVERSE WORK or turn work upside down.

12

METHOD OF WORKING

The art of tatting is moving the shuttle forwards and backwards, under and over the thread around the left hand. The fingers of the left hand, especially the second finger, must be relaxed while the thread to the shuttle in the right hand is pulled tight. When this is mastered, tatting becomes both easy and relaxing.

MAKING THE STITCHES

The first half of the double stitch

Fill the shuttle with cotton, the thread to come out at the top left hand side and where the shuttle has a hook this should face left. Pull 12" to 15" of thread from the shuttle. Take the thread about 2" from the end between the thumb and first finger of the left hand. Pass the thread around all the fingers to make a circle, and hold securely under the thumb. Space the first and second fingers about 2" apart. Bend the little finger to hold the thread firmly. It is with this thread that the knots are formed.

Hold the shuttle in the right hand in an upright position, thumb to the front and first finger to the back, as in Photo 2A. To make the first

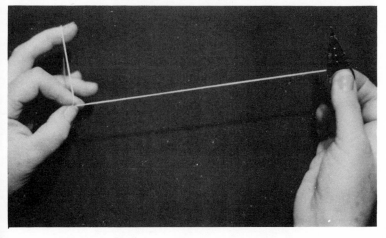

2A

half of the double stitch, bend the last three fingers of the right hand forward over the thread coming from the shuttle. Bring the right hand forward and downward, and with the first finger on top of the shuttle

13

and the cotton raised on the middle finger, slide the shuttle under the thread between the first and second fingers of the left hand with the thread passing between the shuttle and first finger until the back point of the shuttle has passed the thread that is around the hand. Lift the shuttle above the thread and bring it out, the thread passing between the shuttle and the thumb, as in Photo 2B. Gently relax the fingers of the left hand, and at the same time firmly pull the shuttle thread until it is in a horizontal position. Keep the right hand still until the knot has formed on top of the shuttle thread; now slowly extend the second finger

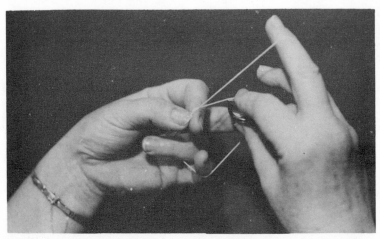

2B

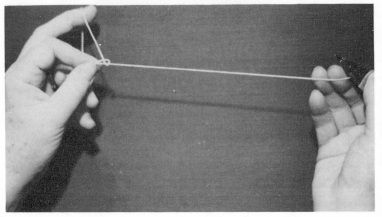

2C

14

of the left hand, thus sliding the loop into position until it is held firmly between the thumb and first finger of the left hand, as in Photo 2c. This is where practice is needed to form the loops correctly with the thread on the left hand. If the loop is formed by the shuttle thread, then this will form a knot and the loops will not draw up into a ring. The secret is to relax the fingers of the left hand, while the shuttle comes from over the thread, holding them in this position until the shuttle is drawn firmly to the right, then lifting the second finger and sliding the loop along the shuttle thread.

The second half of the double stitch
Slide the shuttle forward over the top of the thread, as in Photo 2D,

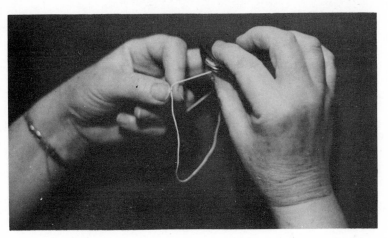

2D

the thread passing between the thumb and the shuttle, until the back point of the shuttle has passed over the thread between the fingers. Drop the back of the shuttle down, and bring it out. Relax the fingers of the left hand and at the same time firmly pull the shuttle thread until it is in a horizontal position. Keep the right hand still until the knot has formed on the top of the shuttle thread; now slowly extend the second finger of the left hand, thus sliding the loop into position close against the first half of the stitch under the thumb, as in Photo 2E.

These two halves form the double stitch used throughout tatting.

15

2E

As the thread around the left hand is used up by the knots, more may be obtained by gently pulling on the bottom thread that is between the thumb and little finger of the left hand. At the same time draw a little more thread from the shuttle, but do not have more than about 8″ of thread between the hands.

As each double stitch is formed, slide it along the thread until it rests against the preceding double stitch, and, when sufficient of these have been worked, they can be pulled up into a ring. To do this, hold all the double stitches firmly between the thumb and first finger of the left hand and pull hard on the shuttle thread until the ring is completely closed. Then give it another pull to make sure that the ring is as tight as you can possibly get it.

TO MAKE PICOTS

Picots are the small loops of thread worked around the rings and on the chains, which enable them to be joined together. They add greatly to the beauty of the work and give greater variety of design.

To make a ring or chain with picots

Work one or more double stitches, then make the first half of a double stitch and slide it to within $\frac{1}{4}″$ of the preceding double stitch. Photo 3A.

Hold it in this position until the second half of the stitch has been worked and slide the two together close to the previous stitches. Photo 3B. The loop so formed is a picot. The size of the picot may be

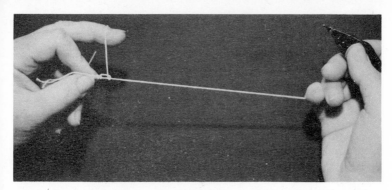

3A

3B

altered by adjusting the length of the thread between the stitches. With thicker cotton a longer length of thread is needed for the picot.

A little practice will soon give proficiency in obtaining picots of even length. When several rings with picots evenly spaced have been made, practise joining the rings together to make a simple edging.

Picots worked over a piece of card

This method is invaluable when several picots of even length are required, or when picots are needed to be worked in echelon.

To make them, work the required number of ds as given in the pattern. Take a piece of thin card approximately 3″ long and as wide as twice the length of the picot about to be formed. Place the card close to the last double stitch, with the thread that is around the hand at the back of the card and the thread from the shuttle in front of the card, proceed to make the next double stitch.

Remove the card, slide the double stitch close to the previous double stitch and continue in pattern.

To Join the Rings

To join the rings or chains, insert the hook on the end of the shuttle (or in the case of a plastic shuttle, a fine crochet hook) downwards through the picot, picking up, from right to left, the thread that is around the left hand. Pull this through the picot and pass the shuttle through the loop, and firmly out to the right. With the second finger of the left hand ease the loop along the horizontal shuttle thread, until it lies evenly against the previous double stitch. Pull the shuttle thread gently to make sure that the stitch is correctly made and that the rings will pull up.

Complete the ring as before.

All joins of rings and chains are made in this way.

The Half Ring

This is a method of enabling the tatter to get from one row of rings to another row of rings without using a short length of thread, the ring being only pulled up halfway. This ring can be made of any number of double stitches, but not less than 6, and great care should be taken to pull the ring up only halfway, so that the thread not covered by the stitches is lying quite straight and taut between the first and last double stitches. This is a very effective way of going from one row of rings across to another row of rings. This of course, gives the edging more strength, which is shown to advantage in the pattern for the Lady's Choker (page 102).

The Mock Ring

This is really a chain, used to form a ring. It is made by joining the end of a chain to the beginning of a chain by means of a very small picot made at the commencement of the chain.

The Chain

A chain is made by using two separate threads, one thread from the shuttle and the other from the ball, although in some patterns where two shuttles are used both threads will come from shuttles.

Many patterns can be made using the chain only, and in this book some will appear as simple edgings, while others form the centre of

18

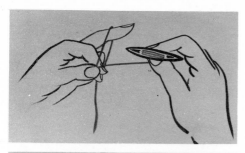

Diagram 1
Holding thread around
the left hand

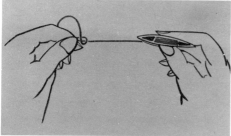

Diagram 2
Completion of first
half of double stitch

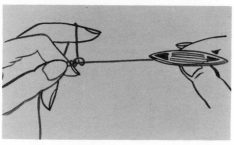

Diagram 3
Completion of
double stitch

Diagram 4
Completion of ring
with picots

19

mats. A continuous chain can form the centre of medallions, and this is worked in the form of a spiral, the chains being held together by tiny picots. These spiral chains are worked in the centre of the glass mats and the medallions on the linen handbag. More decorative edgings can be achieved by using chains in blocks, each chain being held to the next by picots at each end of the block, and such a pattern can be found on the Summer Handbag (page 94).

TATTING WITH TWO THREADS

The shuttle thread only is used when a design is comprised entirely of rings.

Shuttle thread and ball thread are used for working chains or bars; these are not pulled up into rings.

Two threads can also come from two shuttles. These are chiefly used when rings are needed in the centre of chains, or when working the josephine knot on a chain. Several patterns appear in this book for using two shuttles.

It is a good plan when practising with two threads, to have one colour in the shuttle and another colour in the ball.

When commencing work with a shuttle and ball, first fill the shuttle with cotton, but do not cut it off from the ball. Make a ring as previously directed, turn it downwards, and take up the thread from the ball. Pass this thread across the fingers of the left hand, and twist it round the little finger to hold it firm. Take up the shuttle to work the stitches on the thread that lies across the left hand. Make the first half of the double stitch and slide it along the thread as close as possible to the ring, make the second half of the stitch. When all the double stitches have been made on this thread, pull on the thread to tighten the stitches.

Having completed a ring and a chain, remove the ball thread from the left hand, turn the work again upwards, so that the ring is on top and the chain below. Make another ring, sliding the first half of the stitch as close as possible to the last stitch of the previous chain. Join the ring to the previous ring by the picot, as previously described, and complete the ring to match the last one. Turn the work again, to make the next chain. This is called 'reversing the work'.

WEAVING IN OF THREADS

This is the technique used throughout this book to avoid starting the work by tying the threads together into a knot. It is also used to join in new threads in the course of the work.

20

When commencing work with a shuttle and ball (where it is not possible to leave the thread attached to the ball) first make a ring as previously directed. When the ring is drawn up, turn it downwards, and join on the ball thread by passing it though the ring just made, pulling it firmly between the first and last stitches of the ring. Tie with a single knot, this knot can form the first half of the following double stitch, thus avoiding an extra half stitch in the chain to follow. Two ends are now facing upwards, and these must be woven in to avoid loose ends, which look untidy and in time would fray and possibly become untied.

With the ball thread across the fingers of the left hand, make the first half of the double stitch, but before sliding it along the thread up to the ring, pull the two loose ends of thread through this stitch, the threads following the shuttle thread. Hold all three threads securely between the thumb and first finger of the right hand and slide the first half of the double stitch as close as possible to the base of the ring. Make the second half of the double stitch and again pass the two loose ends of thread through the stitch, hold securely and slide the second half of the stitch close to the first half. When these two ends have passed through three double stitches, cut them off as close as possible, leaving no ends. When the pattern allows, one end can be cut off after three double stitches, and the other after four, thus tapering down the thickness. Photo 4.

4

To join ball and shuttle thread to a picot on a chain
Pull both threads through the picot, tie with a single knot, this knot to form the first half of the following double stitch, and proceed as before.

When the pattern is for rings only, commence the ring with one double stitch, fold back the loose end, and weave this in.

When joining on a new thread while working in rings only, leave a length of thread after the last ring worked.

Make the first ring on the new thread as before. Tie the thread left from the last ring, leaving the required length of thread between the rings, to the base of the ring just made. Thread a needle with the thread and overcast neatly along the side of the ring.

The same rules apply to the joining of threads in the course of work, always making the join, whether from ball or shuttle thread, after a ring. Except where the work consists of chains only when the new thread to be taken into use, either from the ball or the shuttle, is joined to the same picot as the last chain, knotted to itself, this knot to form the first half of the stitch as before.

This movement will be referred to in all the patterns in this book as 'weaving in'.

JOSEPHINE KNOT

The jospehine knot consists of a number of single stitches, namely the first or second half of the double stitch. These knots can be made of five or six stitches, pulled up to form a small firm knot, or of ten or twelve stitches to make a larger, softer knot.

These knots can provide extra decoration on the edges of chains or in the centre of rings.

Two shuttles are required while working the josephine knot, but full directions are given in the patterns in this book where these knots are made.

To work an edging of rings directly on to the hem of a handkerchief
This hem must be very narrow, preferably not more than $\frac{1}{8}''$.

Fill the shuttle with thread and attach the end to the handkerchief by inserting the hook of the shuttle, or a crochet hook, as the case may be, into the first hole of the hemstitching to the right of any corner, and pulling a loop of thread through. Pass the shuttle through this loop and draw up the stitch until the knot lies neatly on the edge of the hem.

Make a small ring of 3ds, 3ps, sep by 3ds, 3ds, cl, and join again to the hem as before missing one hole of the hemstitching. Join again into the next hole. Make another ring as before, joining to the last picot of the previous ring and continue all round the handkerchief. Here the tatter must use her own judgment as to how many stitches need to be worked between each ring in order to keep the work lying flat.

For left-handed people

No difficulty will be experienced by left-handed people in learning to tat, as directions for each stitch apply to both right- and left-handed. The left-handed work from right to left, and a mirror placed to the left of the pictures will be a great help.

MOUNTINGS AND FINISHINGS

To insert a medallion into a mat

Place the finished medallion in the correct position on the linen and firmly tack in place. Mark a faint pencil line around the medallion about one thread away from the picots. Work buttonhole stitch, picking up approximately three threads above the pencil line and with the needle coming out on the pencil line, make the knots of the buttonhole stitch against the edge of the tatting. Catch in the picots as you come to them. Remove the tacking and cut away the linen from the back of the medallion using a small but sharp pair of scissors.

To apply tatting to the edge of a mat

a. This can be done as previously described in which case the linen needs to be about $\frac{1}{2}''$ larger all round than the tatting.
b. Hem or hemstitch the mat and apply the tatting by picking up two threads on the edge of the mat with the picot and running the needle through the hem to the position of the next picot.

To frame a medallion

Cut a piece of stiff card slightly smaller than the inside measurements of the frame. Cut a piece of material about 1″ larger all round than the card, but in the case of miniatures, this could be a little less. With a needle threaded with a long length of strong cotton, work a lacing stitch from top to bottom and from side to side, pulling the material taut over the cardboard. After pressing the medallion, tack it in the correct place on the material, only a few stitches being required.

Edging on lampshades

The tatted edging needs to be a little shorter than the distance round the lampshade, so that a good fit results. All shades should be bound top and bottom before putting on the edging and the stitch used to attach the edging is the same diagonal stitch used to stitch on braid.

23

FINISHINGS

After following the instructions given in this book no knots, except the last one, should appear on any piece of tatting. Tie the final knot, thread a needle with one end and overcast neatly over the top of 3ds to the left and with the other thread repeat, but to the right.

LAUNDERING

Great care should be taken when pressing tatting and rustless pins should be used to pin the work to the right size and shape. Pin all chains at the centre to get the right curve and by the centre picot of the outside rings.

Always press with a very damp cloth and fairly hot iron.

All tatting that is to be applied to a finished article, such as buttons, collars, bags, dresses, etc., must be pressed first.

Handkerchief edging No. 1

Materials: Coats Mercer-Crochet No. 60. 1 ball white, but any other shade may be used. Tatting shuttle. Handkerchief.

This handkerchief edging is worked with shuttle thread only, which is joined to the handkerchief ⅛″ to the right of any corner.

1st Ring. 4ds, p. 4ds, p, 1ds, p, 4ds, p, 4ds, cl. Join by shuttle thread to hem of handkerchief, and work twice more into hem.

2nd Ring. 4ds, join to adjacent p of 1st r, 4ds, p, 1ds, p, 4ds, p, 4ds, cl. Join by shuttle thread to hem of handkerchief, and work twice more into hem. (These stitches into hem may be varied in order to keep the work even.)

Repeat 2nd r along one side, taking care to finish the last r ⅛″ from corner. Work one r on corner, and next r ⅛″ away on next side of handkerchief.

Repeat along the other three sides and join last p of last r to first p of 1st r. Cut thread and overcast neatly on to edge of handkerchief.

25

Handkerchief edging No. 2

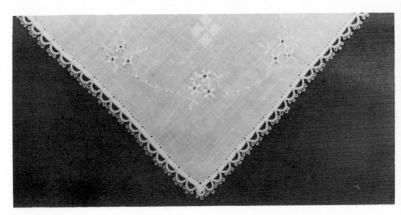

Materials: Coats Mercer-Crochet No. 60. 1 ball white, but any other shade may be used. Tatting shuttle. Handkerchief.

This handkerchief edging is worked with shuttle and ball thread, which is joined to handkerchief ⅛" to the right of any corner.

1st Chain. 4ds, 3ps, sep by 2ds, 4ds, join by shuttle thread to handkerchief ¼" along hem.

Repeat this ch to within ⅛" of next corner.

Repeat same ch and join by shuttle thread ⅛" from corner on next side.

Repeat all around handkerchief, joining last ch to same place as 1st ch. Cut ends and stitch neatly into handkerchief.

Handkerchief edging No. 3

Materials: Coats Mercer-Crochet No. 40. 1 ball beige 608. Pale green linen handkerchief. Tatting shuttle.

This edging is worked in shuttle thread only, and $\frac{1}{8}''$ length of thread is left between all rs.

1st Ring. *4ds, p, 4ds, cl. RW.
2nd Ring. 4ds, 3ps sep by 4ds, 4ds, cl. RW.
3rd Ring. 4ds, join to p of 1st r, 2ds, 4ps sep by 2ds, 4ds, cl. RW.
4th Ring. 4ds, join to adjacent p of 2nd r, 4ds, p, 4ds, p, 4ds, cl. RW.
5th Ring. 4ds, join to last p of 3rd r, 4ds, cl. RW.
6th Ring. As 4th.
Repeat from * until length required for one side of handkerchief ending with 5th r.
Repeat 5th r again, followed by 2nd r.
A corner has been made by missing out 6th r.
Repeat all around handkerchief, joining last p of 4th r to 1st p of 2nd r and still leaving $\frac{1}{8}''$ length of thread, join to base of 1st r. Cut thread, and overcast neatly to 1st r. Press with a damp cloth and warm iron.

Handkerchief edging No. 4

Materials: Coats Mercer-Crochet No. 60. 1 ball white. Handkerchief. Tatting shuttle.

This edging is worked in shuttle thread only.

1st Ring. 6ds, p, 2ds, 5ps sep by 2ds, 6ds, cl. Leave approx. $\frac{1}{4}''$ length of thread.
2nd Ring. *6ds, join to last p of previous r, 1ds, p, 6ds, cl. Leave approx $\frac{1}{4}''$ length of thread.

3rd Ring. 6ds, join to last p of previous r, 2ds, 5ps sep by 2ds, 6ds, cl. Leave approx. $\frac{1}{4}''$ length of thread.
Repeat from * until length required for one side of handkerchief.
Corner, repeat 3rd r again. Work 3 more sides to match, joining last p of 3rd r to 1st p of 1st r.
Stitch edging to handkerchief by the thread connecting the rs. Press with damp cloth and warm iron.

Handkerchief edging No. 5

Materials: Coats Mercer-Crochet No. 60. 1 ball white. Handkerchief. Tatting shuttle.

This edging is worked in shuttle thread only, with ⅛″ length of thread left between all rings.

1st Ring. *3ds, 3ps sep by 3ds, 3ds, cl. RW. Leave ⅛″ length of thread.

2nd Ring. 4ds, p, 3ds, p, 4ds, cl. RW. Leave ⅛″ length of thread.

3rd Ring. 3ds, join to last p of 1st r, 3ds, p, 3ds, p, 3ds, cl. RW. Leave ⅛″ length of thread.

4th Ring. 4ds, join to 2nd p of 2nd r, 2ds, 4ps sep by 2ds, 4ds, cl. RW.

Repeat from * joining rings together as before, until length required for side of handkerchief, finishing after 4th r.

Repeat 4th r again, and then repeat from *. Work three other sides to match, joining last p of 3rd r to 1st p of 1st r, and last p of 2nd 4th r to 1st p of 2nd r. Cut thread and join to top of 1st r, oversew neatly. Press with damp cloth and warm iron.

Handkerchief edging in pink No. 6

Materials: Coats Mercer-Crochet No. 40. 1 ball pink 503. Pale blue linen handkerchief. Tatting shuttle.

1st Ring. 6ds, p, 6ds, cl.
2nd Ring. 6ds, p, 6ds, close beside 1st r, cl. RW.
1st Chain. Tie cotton to 1st r and weave in ends. 8ds. RW.
3rd Ring. 6ds, join to p of 2nd r, 6ds cl.
4th Ring. As 2nd r.
2nd Chain. 2ds, 5ps sep by 2ds, 2ds. RW.
Repeat from * to corner, finishing after 2nd ch.

Ring. 6ds, join to p of previous r, 6ds, cl. RW.
Chain. As previous ch. RW.
Ring. As 1st r, joining to p where previous 2 rs were joined.
3 rs for corner.
Repeat to match 1st side, all around handkerchief, joining p of 4th r to p of 1st r.
Work last corner to match.
Cut threads and fasten to base of 1st 2 rs. Tie and overcast neatly. Stitch edging to handkerchief by picots joining rings. Press with damp cloth and warm iron.

Handkerchief edging with josephine knots No. 7

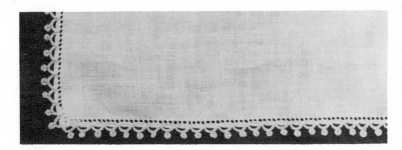

Materials: Coats Mercer-Crochet No. 40. 1 ball turquoise 521. Pink linen handkerchief. 2 tatting shuttles.

This edging is worked directly on to the handkerchief. Fasten threads to handkerchief, and weave in on first chain.

1st Chain. *With shuttle No. 1 4ds. With shuttle No. 2 work a josephine knot of 9 first half knots, cl. With 1st shuttle 4ds. Fasten by 1st shuttle thread to hand-

kerchief, leaving enough space for the chain to arch nicely.

Repeat from * along 1st side of handkerchief.

No definite pattern can be given for corners, as this will depend on the number of holes along the side of the handkerchief, but endeavour to work each corner to match. Cut threads and fasten to the handkerchief at the base of the 1st ch. Press with damp cloth and warm iron.

Elegant handkerchief edging No. 8

Materials: Coats Mercer-Crochet No. 60. 1 ball white. Handkerchief. Tatting shuttle.

1st Ring. *3ds, 6ps sep by 3ds, 3ds, cl. RW.
1st Chain. 3ds, 4ps sep by 3ds, 3ds, RW.
2nd Ring. 3ds, p, 3ds, join to 2nd last p of previous r, 3ds, 4ps sep by 3ds, 3ds, cl. RW.
2nd Chain. As 1st ch RW.
3rd Ring. 3ds, 2ps sep by 3ds, 3ds, join to 2nd last p of previous r, 3ds, 2ps, sep by 3ds, 3ds, cl.
4th Ring. Close beside previous r,

3ds, 5ps sep by 3ds, 3ds, cl. RW.
3rd Chain. As 1st ch
Repeat from * to corner finishing after 2nd ch.

CORNER CLOVER
1st Ring. As 3rd r.
2nd Ring. 3ds, join to last p of previous r, 3ds, 4ps, sep by 3ds, 3ds, cl.
3rd Ring. As previous r.
Chain. As previous ch.
Work other 3 sides to match and joining 3rd p of last r of clover to 2nd p of 1st r and joining last ch to base of 1st r.

Fine dainty handkerchief for special occasions No. 9

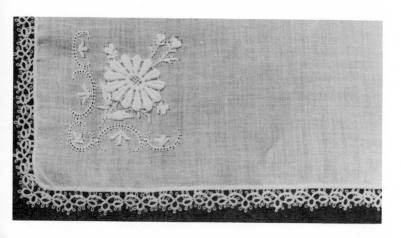

Materials: Coats Mercer-Crochet No. 100. 1 ball white. Fine linen handkerchief. Tatting shuttle.

1st Ring. 3ds, 5ps sep by 3ds, 3ds, cl. RW.
1st Chain. Join to base of 1st r, and

weave in ends. 4ds, 3ps, sep by 4ds, 4ds, RW.
2nd Ring. *3ds, p, 3ds, p, 3ds, join to last p of previous r, 3ds, p, 3ds, p, 3ds, cl.
3rd Ring. Close beside previous r. 3ds, 5ps sep by 3ds, 3ds, cl. RW.

31

2nd Chain. As 1st ch.
4th Ring. 3ds, join to centre p of previous r, 3ds, 4ps sep by 3ds, 3ds, cl. RW.
3rd Chain. As 1st ch.
Repeat from * until sufficient for one side of handkerchief, finishing after 1st r.
Work a similar r beside the previous r, joining 1st p to last p of previous r, cl. RW.
Chain. As before.
Repeat from * and work 3 other sides of handkerchief to match, joining last r to 1st r.
Cut threads and join to base of 1st r, overcast neatly. Stitch to handkerchief. Press with damp cloth and warm iron.

Another handkerchief for that special occasion No. 10

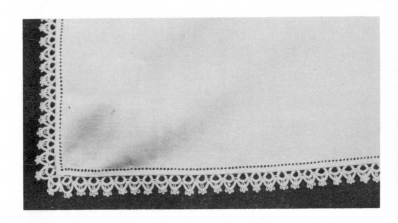

Materials: Coats Mercer-Crochet No. 60. 1 ball white. 1 linen handkerchief. Tatting shuttle.

1st ROW
With shuttle thread only, leaving ¼″ length of threads between all rs.
1st Ring. 4ds, 3ps sep by 4ds, 4ds, cl.
2nd Ring. 4ds, join to last p of previous r, 4ds, p, 4ds, p, 4ds, cl.
Repeat this r until sufficient to go all around handkerchief, joining last p of last r to 1st p of 1st r.

2nd ROW
1st Chain. Join threads to p joining two rs together and weave in ends. 6ds, 3ps sep by 1ds, 6ds, join by shuttle thread to p, joining 2 rs together.
Repeat to end, joining last ch to base of 1st ch. Cut threads, tie and overcast neatly. Stitch to handkerchief by thread joining rings. Press with damp cloth and warm iron.

Handkerchief edging or Pillow edging No. 11

Materials: Coats Mercer-Crochet No. 60. 1 ball white. Tatting shuttle.

1st Ring. 4ds, p, 4ds, p, 4ds, p, 4ds, cl. RW. Join ball thread to r and weave in ends.

1st Chain. 6ds, p, 6ds. RW.

2nd Ring. *6ds, join to last p of 1st r, 3ds, p, 3ds, cl. RW.

2nd Chain. 10ds, RW.

3rd Ring. 3ds, join to 2nd p of previous r, 3ds, p, 6ds, cl. RW.

3rd Chain. 6ds, p, 6ds. RW.

4th Ring. 4ds, join to 2nd p of previous r, 4ds, join to 2nd p of 1st r, 4ds, p, 4ds, cl. DO NOT REVERSE WORK.

4th Chain. 6ds. DO NOT REVERSE WORK.

5th Ring. 4ds, p, 4ds, p, 4ds, p, 4ds, cl. RW.

5th Chain. 6ds, join to p of opposite ch, 6ds. RW.

Repeat from * for length required to corner, finishing after 4th ch.

CORNER

1st Ring. 4ds, p, 4ds, p, 2ds, p, 4ds, p, 4ds, cl. RW.

1st Chain. 6ds, join to p of opposite ch, 6ds. RW.

2nd Ring. 6ds, join to last p of previous r, 3ds, p, 3ds, cl. RW.

2nd Chain. 10ds, RW.

3rd Ring. 4ds, join to 2nd p of previous r, 4ds, join to 3rd p of 1st r, 2ds, p, 4ds, p, 4ds, cl. RW.

3rd Chain. 10ds, RW.

4th Ring. 3ds, join to 4th p of previous r, 3ds, p, 6ds, cl. RW.

4th Chain. 6ds, p, 6ds, RW.

5th Ring. 4ds, join to 2nd p of previous r, 4ds, join to 3rd p of 3rd r, 2ds, join to 2nd p of 1st r, 4ds, p, 4ds, cl. DO NOT REVERSE WORK.

5th Chain. 6ds. DO NOT REVERSE WORK.

6th Ring. 4ds, p, 4ds, p, 4ds, p, 4ds, cl. RW.

6th Chain. 6ds, join to p of opposite ch, 6ds. RW.

Repeat from * all around handkerchief, finishing last corner by joining p of 4th ch to p of 1st ch, and 5th ch to base of 1st r. Cut ends and overcast neatly. Stitch to handkerchief and press with damp cloth and warm iron.

Handkerchief edging or edging for Place Mat No. 12

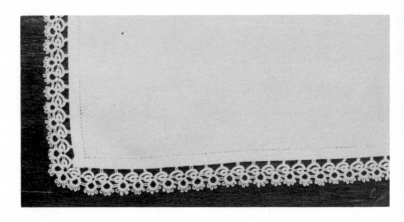

Materials: Coats Mercer-Crochet No. 60 for handkerchief or 20 for place mat. Handkerchief. 1 ball white, or any other colour may be used. Tatting shuttle.

1st Ring. *4ds, 6p sep by 2ds, 4ds, cl.
2nd Ring. Close to 1st r. 4ds, p, 4ds, cl. RW.
1st Chain. 5ds, p, 5ds, join by shuttle thread to p of 2nd r. RW.
Repeat from * joining 1st p of 2nd large r, to last p of previous large r.

Repeat for length required to corner, finishing after 1st r.
Repeat 1st r again, followed by 2nd r, thus forming a corner.
Repeat all around handkerchief; on last corner, join last p of previous large r to 1st p of 1st r. cl.
Join p of small r to base of 1st r and ch to same place. Cut threads and join to base of 1st r, tie, overcast neatly.

Edging worked in Sylko directly on to the handkerchief

Orange mat with contrast edging

Materials: Coats Mercer-Crochet No. 20. 1 ball dark brown 579. 2 tatting shuttles. Orange linen mat $18\frac{1}{2}'' \times 13\frac{1}{2}''$. Fill 1st shuttle with cotton and draw sufficient from ball to fill 2nd shuttle without cutting cotton.

1st Ring. With 1st shuttle: *3ds, 7ps, sep by 3ds, 3ds, cl. RW.
1st Chain. 5ds. Do not RW.
2nd Ring. 3ds, 5ps sep by 3ds, 3ds, cl. Do not RW.
2nd Chain. 5ds. RW.
3rd Ring. 3ds p, 3ds, join to 2nd last p of 1st r, 3ds, 5ps sep by 3ds, 3ds, cl. RW.
3rd Chain. 5ds. Do not RW.
4th Ring. 3ds, p, 3ds, join to 2nd

last p of 2nd r, 3ds, 5ps sep by 3ds, 3ds. Do not RW.
4th Chain. 5ds, RW.
5th Ring. As 3rd r, RW.
5th Chain. 5ds. Do not RW.
6th Ring. 3ds, p, 3ds, join to 2nd last p of 4th r, 3ds, 3ps, sep by 3ds, 3ds, cl. Do not RW.
6th Chain. 5ds, RW.
7th Ring. As 5th r. RW.
7th Chain. 7ds, join to last p of 6th r, 3ds, p. 3ds.
With 2nd shuttle make a josephine knot of 12 1st halves of the ds.
With 1st shuttle, 3ds, p, 3ds, p, 7ds. RW.
Repeat from * to 1st corner, adding p, 3ds, to 7th ch, and joining to 2nd p of previous r.

36

CORNER

Chain. 3ds, join to last p of 7th ch, 5ds. Do not RW.

Ring. 3ds, join to next p of 7th ch, 3ds, 4ps sep by 3ds, 3ds, cl. RW.

Chain. 5ds, RW.

Ring. 3ds, p, 3ds, join to 2nd last p of previous r, 3ds, 3ps sep by 3ds, 3ds, cl. Do not RW.

Chain. 5ds, p, 3ds, join to same p as 1st ch.

Chain. 3ds, join to last p of previous ch, 7ds, join to last p of previous r, 3ds, p, 3ds, with 2nd shuttle work a josephine knot, with 1st shuttle 3ds, p, 3ds, p, 7ds.

Repeat from * joining 2nd p of 1st r, to same p as previous chs.

This edging is stitched to the linen with the first row of rs overlapping the linen. This gives an unusual effect. Press with damp cloth and warm iron.

Attractive Long Runner

Materials: Coats Mercer-Crochet No. 20. 1 ball 459. Tatting shuttle. Piece of linen 23″ × 9½″. Measurements: linen mat 21″ × 7½″, overall size 24″ × 10½″.

1st ROW

1st Ring. 5ds, p, 5ds, p, 5ds, p, 5ds, cl. RW.
1st Chain. 4ds, p, 2ds, p, 4ds. RW.
2nd Ring. *5ds, join to last p of 1st r, 5ds, p, 5ds, p, 5ds, cl. RW.
2nd Chain. As 1st ch.
Repeat from * until sufficient for one side of mat finishing after a r, the number of rs to be divisible by 4 plus one.

CORNER

Chain. 4ds. RW.
Ring. 5ds, join to last p of previous r, 5ds, 3 ps sep by 5ds, 5ds, cl. RW.
Chain. 4ds. RW.
Repeat r and ch to next corner. Continue all around, joining last ch to 1st r. Cut threads, tie and overcast neatly.

2nd ROW

1st Ring. *7ds, with 1st row of edging on your left, join to the centre p of second r, after any corner r, 5ds, p, 5ds, p, 7ds, cl. RW.
1st Chain. 6ds, 3ps sep by 2ds, 6ds. RW.
2nd Ring. 7ds, join to last p of previous r, 5ds, p, 5ds, p, 7ds, cl. RW.
2nd Chain. As 1st ch. RW.
3rd Ring. As 2nd r.
3rd Chain. As 1st ch.
4th Ring. As previous r.
4th Chain. As previous ch.
5th Ring. 7ds, join to last p of previous r, 5ds, p, 5ds, join to centre p of 4th r of previous row, 7ds, cl. RW.
5th Chain. 4ds. RW.
6th Ring. 7ds, join to 6th r of previous row, 5ds, p, 5ds, p, 7ds, cl. RW.
6th Chain. 6ds, p, 2ds, join to centre p of 4th ch, 2ds, p, 6ds. RW.
Continue as before, always leaving one free r of previous row between scallops and in centre of scallop.
After 5th ch commence corner.

1st Ring. 7ds, join to 1st free p of corner r, 5ds, p, 5ds, p, 7ds, cl. RW.
1st Chain. As previous ch. RW.
Repeat r and ch until 5 rs and chs have been made.
6th Ring. 7ds, join to last p of previous r, 5ds, p, 5ds, join to next p of corner r, 7ds, cl. RW.

Repeat all around, joining centre p of 4th ch to centre p of lst ch and 5th ch of last repeat to base of 1st r. Cut threads, tie and overcast neatly. Stitch to edge of linen which has been previously hemmed or hemstitched. Press with damp cloth and warm iron.

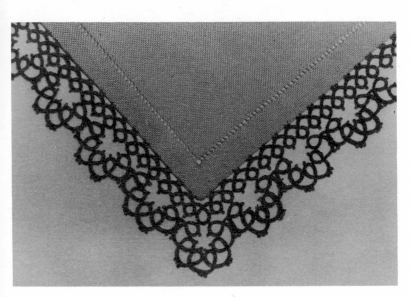

Edging for Luncheon Mats

Materials: Coats Mercer-Crochet No. 20. 2 balls ecru 610, but any other shade may be used. Linen to match, or contrast. Tatting shuttle. Depth of edging 1½″.
Measurements:
Large Mat 12″ diameter.
Small Mat 6″ diameter.

Cut a circle of linen 10″ in diameter and lay a small hem all round. Fill shuttle with cotton but do not cut it off from the ball.
1st Ring. 8ds, p, 8ds, cl.
2nd Ring. As previous r.
3rd Ring. As previous r. RW.
1st Chain. 12ds. Do not RW.

4th Ring. 4ds, 4ps sep by 4ds, 4ds, cl.
2nd Chain. 8ds, p, 8ds, join by shuttle thread to 1st p of previous r.
3rd Chain. 3ds, 3ps sep by 2ds, 3ds, join by shuttle thread to next p of same r.
4th Chain. As previous ch.
5th Chain. As previous ch.
6th Chain. 8ds, p, 8ds, join by shuttle thread to base of r.
7th Chain. *12ds. RW.
5th Ring. 8ds, join to p of last r of 3 r group, 8ds, cl.
6th Ring. 8ds, p, 8ds, cl.
7th Ring. 8ds, p, 8ds, cl. RW.
8th Chain. 12ds.

8th Ring. 4ds, 4ps sep by 4ds, 4ds, cl.

9th Chain. 8ds, join to p of last ch of previous group, 8ds, join by shuttle thread to first p of previous r.

10th Chain. 3ds, join to first p of next ch of previous group, 2ds, 2ps sep by 2ds, 3ds, join by shuttle thread to next p of same r.

11th Chain. 3ds, 3ps sep by 2ds, 3ds, join by shuttle thread to next p of same r.

12th Chain. As previous ch.

13th Chain. 8ds, p, 8ds, join by shuttle thread to base of same r.

Repeat from * until there is sufficient to go all round mat, joining last p of last r of 3 r group to first p of 1st r of first 3 r group and joining ps of ch of large group to corresponding ps, then ch of 12ds, and join to base of first r. Cut threads, tie and overcast neatly.

GLASS MAT

Cut a circle of linen 4″ in diameter and lay a small hem all round. Work edging same as large mat. Press with a damp cloth and warm iron.

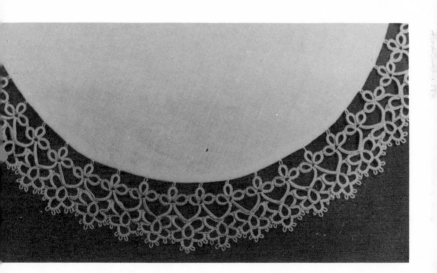

Edging for Table Napkin

Materials: Coats Mercer-Crochet No. 20. 1 ball orange 538. Table napkin, orange, but any other colour could be used. 1 tatting shuttle.

Fill shuttle with cotton but do not cut it off from the ball.
1st Ring. 6ds, p, 6ds, cl. RW.
1st Chain. 6ds, 3ps sep by 2ds, 6ds. RW.
2nd Ring. *6ds, join to p of 1st r, 6ds, cl. Do not RW.

3rd Ring. Close by previous r, 6ds, p, 6ds, cl. RW.
2nd Chain. As 1st ch.
Repeat from * until there is sufficient to go all around napkin, joining last r to base of 1st r. Cut threads, tie and overcast neatly. Stitch to edge of napkin, easing around corners. Press with damp cloth and warm iron.

Tatted Medallions inserted into this Tray Cloth give it an air of distinction

Materials: Coats Mercer-Crochet No. 20. 2 balls ecru 610. ½ yd linen. 1 tatting shuttle.

Measurements: Medallion 3″ square: Tray Cloth 20″ × 15″.

Starting at one corner of medallion, fill shuttle with cotton but do not cut it off from the ball.

1st Ring. 6ds, p, 6ds, cl. RW.

1st Chain. 6ds, 3ps, sep by 2ds, 6ds, p, 6ds, RW.

2nd Ring. 6ds, join to p of previous r, 6ds, cl. RW.

2nd Chain. 6ds. RW.

3rd Ring. 6ds, p, 6ds, cl. RW.

3rd Chain. 6ds. RW.

4th Ring. 6ds, p, 6ds, cl. RW.

4th Chain. 6ds, join to single p of 1st ch, 6ds, 3 ps sep by 2ds, 6ds. RW.

5th Ring. 6ds, join to p of last r, 6ds, cl. RW.

5th Chain. 6ds, 3ps sep by 2ds, 6ds, p, 6ds. RW.

6th Ring. 6ds, join to p where last 2 rs were joined, 6ds, cl. RW.

6th Chain. 6ds, p, 6ds, p, 6ds. RW.

7th Ring. 6ds, join to same p, 6ds, cl. RW. (first motif made).

7th Chain. 6ds. RW.

8th Ring. 6ds, join to p of adjacent r, 6ds, cl. RW.

43

8th Chain. 6ds. RW.

9th Ring. 6ds, p, 6ds, cl. RW.

9th Chain. 6ds, join to next p of adjacent ch, 6ds, p, 6ds. RW.

10th Ring. 6ds, join to p of last r, 6ds, cl. RW.

10th Chain. 6ds. RW.

11th Ring. 6ds, p, 6ds, cl. RW.

11th Chain. 6ds. RW.

12th Ring. 6ds, p, 6ds, cl. RW.

12th Chain. 6ds, join to p of adjacent ch, 6ds, p, 6ds. RW.

13th Ring. 6ds, join to p of last r, 6ds, cl. RW.

13th Chain. 6ds. RW.

14th Ring. 6ds, p, 6ds, cl. RW.

14th Chain. 6ds. RW.

15th Ring. 6ds, p, 6ds, cl. RW.

15th Chain. 6ds, join to p of last p-ch, 6ds, join to free p of adjacent ch of 1st motif, 6ds. RW.

16th Ring. 6ds, join to p of last r, 6ds, cl. RW.

16th Chain. 6ds, join to single p of adjacent ch of 1st motif, 6ds, 3ps sep by 2ds, 6ds. RW.

17th Ring. 6ds, join to p where last 2 rs were joined, 6ds, cl. RW.

17th Chain. 6ds, 3ps sep by 2ds, 6ds, p, 6ds. RW.

18th Ring. 6ds, join to same p, 6ds, cl. RW.

18th Chain. 6ds. RW.

19th Ring. 6ds, join to p of adjacent r, 6ds, cl. RW.

19th Chain. 6ds. RW.

20th Ring. 6ds, p, 6ds, cl. RW.

20th Chain. 6ds, join to single p of adjacent ch, 6ds, 3ps sep by 2ds, 6ds. RW.

21st Ring. 6ds, join to p of last r, 6ds, cl. RW.

21st Chain. 6ds, 5 ps sep by 2ds, 6ds. RW.

22nd Ring. 6ds, join to p where last 2 rs were joined, 6ds, cl. RW.

22nd Chain. 6ds, 3ps sep by 2ds, 6ds, p, 6ds. RW.

23rd Ring. 6ds, join to same p, 6ds, cl. RW.

23rd Chain. 6ds. RW.

24th Ring. 6ds, join to p between next 2 rs (centre motif) 6ds, cl. RW.

24th Chain. 6ds. RW.

25th Ring. 6ds, p, 6ds, cl. RW.

25th Chain. 6ds, join to single p of adjacent ch, 6ds, 3 ps sep by 2ds, 6ds, RW.

26th Ring. 6ds, join to p of last r, 6ds, cl. RW.

26th Chain. 6ds, 3ps sep by 2ds, 6ds, p, 6ds. RW.

27th Ring. 6ds, join to same p where last 2 rs where joined, 6ds, cl. RW.

27th Chain. 6ds, p, 6ds, p, 6ds, RW.

28th Ring. 6ds, join to same p, 6ds, cl. RW.

28th Chain. 6ds. RW.

29th Ring. 6ds, join to p of centre motif, 6ds, cl. RW.

29th Chain. 6ds. RW.

30th Ring. 6ds, join to p between next 2 rs, 6ds, cl. RW.

30th Chain. 6ds, join to next p of adjacent ch, 6ds p, 6ds. RW.

31st Ring. 6ds, join to same p where last r was joined, 6ds, cl. RW.

31st Chain. 6ds. RW.

32nd Ring, 6ds, join to p of adjacent r, 6ds, cl. RW.

32nd Chain. 6ds. RW.

33rd Ring. 6ds, p, 6ds, cl. RW.

33rd Chain. 6ds, join to p of adjacent ch, 6ds, p, 6ds. RW.

34th Ring. 6ds, join to p of last r, 6ds, cl. RW.

34th Chain. 6ds. RW.

35th Ring. 6ds, p, 6ds, cl. RW.

35th Chain. 6ds. RW.

36th Ring. 6ds, p, 6ds, cl. RW.

36th Chain. 6ds, join to p of last p-ch, 6ds, join to next free p, 6ds RW.

37th Ring. 6ds, join to p of last r, 6ds. cl. RW.

37th Chain. 6ds, join to single p of adjacent ch, 6ds, 3ps sep by 2ds, 6ds. RW.

38th Ring. 6ds, join to p where last 2 rs were joined, 6ds, cl. RW.

38th Chain. 6ds, 3 ps sep by 2ds, 6ds, p, 6ds. RW.

39th Ring. 6ds, join to same p, 6ds, cl. RW.

39th Chain. 6ds. RW.

40th Ring. 6ds, join to p of adjacent r, 6ds, cl. RW.

40th Chain. 6ds. RW.

41st Ring. 6ds, p, 6ds, cl. RW.

41st Chain. 6ds, join to single p of adjacent ch, 6ds, 3ps sep by 2ds, 6ds, RW.

42nd Ring. 6ds, join to p of adjacent r, 6ds, cl.

42nd Chain. 6ds, 5ps sep by 2ds, 6ds. This completes one half of the medallion. Work second half to match. Cut threads, tie and overcast neatly.

EDGING FOR THE MAT

1st Ring. *6ds, p, 6ds, cl. RW.

1st Chain. 6ds, 3ps sep by 2ds, 6ds. RW.

2nd Ring. 6ds, join to p of 1st r, 6ds, cl. RW.

Repeat from * for length required. On corner chains work 5ps instead of 3. Join last r to base of 1st r, cut threads, tie and overcast neatly. Insert the medallions into the cloth following the instructions given in the section 'Mountings and Finishings'. Stitch edging to cloth by the connecting picot between the rings.

45

Child's Collar of Flowers

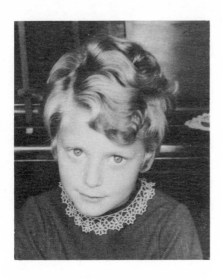

Materials: Coats Mercer-Crochet No. 40. 1 ball blue 594. Tatting shuttle.

1st FLOWER
1st Petal 9ds, p, 8ds, p, 9ds, cl.
2nd Petal. *9ds, join to adjacent p of previous petal, 4ds, p, 4ds, p, 9ds, cl. Repeat from * 5 times more. RW.
Stem. Attach ball thread to base of 1st r, and weave in ends. 14ds. RW.
1st Leaf. 12ds, join to last p of last petal, 5ds, p, 9ds, cl. RW.
2nd Leaf. 12ds, p, 5ds, p, 9ds. Do not RW.
Stem. 10ds, p, 10ds, p, 5ds, p, 10ds. RW.

2nd FLOWER
1st Petal. 9ds, join to last p of previous stem (pull p over stem), 8ds, p, 9ds, cl.
2nd Petal. 9ds, join to adjacent p of previous petal, 4ds, join to p of adjacent leaf, 4ds, p, 9ds, cl.
3rd Petal. 9ds, join to adjacent p of previous petal, 4ds, join to p of last petal of previous flower, 4ds, p, 9ds, cl.
Complete flower to match 1st flower. Repeat for length required joining 1st p of 2nd leaf to adjacent p of stem.

Edging Chain
Join threads to last p of last petal and make chains joining to all the ps on the stems and leaves along the edge of the collar.
Cut threads, tie and oversew neatly. Press with damp cloth and warm iron.

46

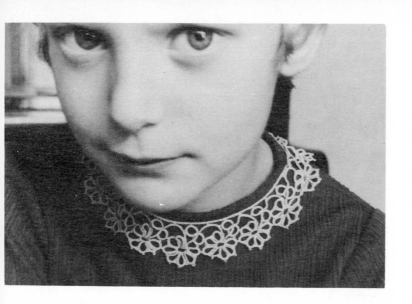

Pretty Collar of Flowers

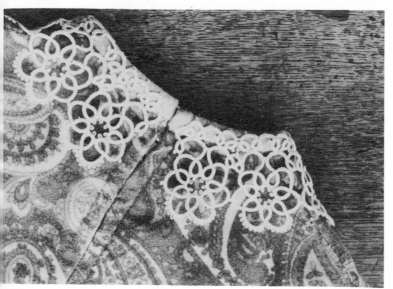

Materials: Coats Mercer-Crochet No. 20. 1 ball turquoise 521. Tatting shuttle.

These pretty flower-like medallions are joined together by chains, and this border would look equally well as an edging for mats, with the chains and rings made a little larger for the top edging.

Fill the shuttle with the cotton but do not cut the thread off from the ball.

1st ROW

1st Ring. 6ds, p, 2ds, p, 6ds, cl. RW.
1st Chain.* 6ds, p, 2ds, p, 6ds, p, 8ds. Do not RW.
2nd Ring. 9ds, p,2 ds, p, 2ds, p 9ds, cl. RW.
2nd Chain. 8ds, p, 8ds. RW.
3rd Ring. 9ds, join to last p of adjacent r, 2ds, p, 2ds, p, 9ds, cl. RW.
3rd Chain. As 2nd ch. RW.
4th Ring. As 3rd r. RW.
4th Chain. 2ds, 9ps, sep by 2ds, 2ds, RW.
5th Ring. As 3rd r.
5th Chain. As previous ch. RW.
6th Ring. As 3rd r. RW.
6th Chain. 8ds, p, 8ds. RW.
7th Ring. As 3rd r. RW.
7th Chain. 8ds, p, 8ds. RW.
8th Ring. 9ds, join to last p of previous r, 2ds, p, 2ds, join to 1st p of 1st r, 9ds, cl. Do not RW.

8th Chain. 8ds. join to p of 1st ch, 6ds, p, 2ds, p, 6ds. RW.
9th Ring. 6ds, join to p of 7th ch, 2ds, p, 6ds, cl. RW.
9th Chain. 4ds, p, 4ds. RW.
10th Ring. 6ds, join to p of previous r, 2ds, p, 6ds, cl. RW.
Repeat from * 10 times more and finishing last repeat at the 9th r. Do not RW and make a turning ch of 6ds, p, 6ds. RW to commence next row.

2nd ROW

1st Ring. 3ds, p, 3ds, join to 1st p of last ch of previous row, 6ds, cl. RW.
1st Chain. 4ds, p, 4ds. RW.
2nd Ring. 6ds, join to 2nd p of same ch, 3ds, p, 3ds, cl. RW.
2nd Chain. 4ds, p, 4ds. RW.
3rd Ring. *3ds, p, 3ds, join to 1st p of next ch, 6ds, cl. RW.
3rd Chain. 4ds, p, 4ds. RW.
4th Ring. 6ds, join to 2nd p of same ch, 3ds, p, 3ds, cl.
5th Ring. 3ds, p, 3ds, missing one ch, join to 1st p of next ch 6ds, cl. RW.
4th Chain. 4ds, p, 4ds. RW.
6th Ring. 6ds, join to next p of same ch, 3ds, p, 3ds, cl. RW.
5th Chain. 4ds, p, 4ds. RW.
Repeat from * to end, joining last turning ch to base of 1st r. Cut threads, tie and overcast neatly. Press with damp cloth and warm iron.

Tiny Flowers for a Little Girl's Dress

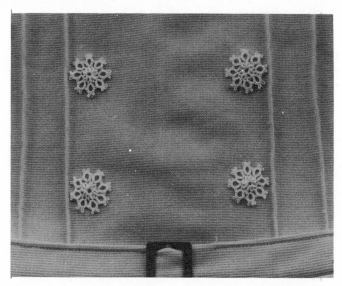

Materials: Coats Mercer-Crochet No. 60. 1 ball white, or any other colour may be used. Tatting shuttle.

These small medallions are worked with shuttle only. They would look very pretty scattered over a summer dress, or as a decoration round the base of a lampshade.

1st Ring. 1ds, fold back the end and weave it in, 3ds, long p, 4ds, cl. RW.

2nd Ring. 4ds, p, 3ds, p 1ds, p, 1ds, p, 3ds, p, 4ds, cl. RW.

3rd Ring. 4ds, join to long p, 4ds, cl. RW.

4th Ring. 4ds, join to last p of 2nd r, 3ds, p, 1ds, p, 1ds, p, 3ds, p, 4ds, cl. RW.

Repeat until there are 8 large rs and 8 small rs, joining the last p of the last large r to the first p of the first large r.

Cut the thread and tie to the base of the first small r and leave sufficient thread to sew the medallion to the dress. Press with a damp cloth and warm iron.

Cake Frill and Napkin Ring

Materials: Coats Mercer-Crochet No. 20. 1 ball orange 538, 1 ball beige 609, but any other two shades may be used. Tatting shuttle.

With beige in shuttle and orange in ball.

1st ROW

1st Ring. 4ds, p, 4ds, p, 4ds, p, 4ds, cl. RW.

1st Chain. 4ds, p, 4ds, p, 4ds, p, 4ds. RW.

2nd Ring. *As 1st r, joining 2nd p to 2nd p of 1st r, cl. RW.

3rd Ring. As 1st r, working close to 2nd r, cl. RW.

2nd Chain. As 1st ch, Repeat from *

for length required finishing after 2nd r. RW.

3rd Chain. 4ds, p, 4ds, p, 4ds, p, 4ds. RW.

2nd ROW

1st Ring. As previous rs, joining 2nd p to centre p of previous 2 rs, cl. RW.

1st Chain. As previous chs. RW.

2nd Ring. As previous rs, joining 2nd p to centre p of previous 3 rs.

Repeat joining rs into groups of 4 to the end.

Make 2nd end to match 1st end.

Join last ch to base of 1st r. Cut ends, tie, and overcast neatly.

50

OUTER ROW

As 1st row, joining 2nd p of ch to centre p of ch of 1st row. Repeat to end, finishing with 2nd r. DO NOT REVERSE WORK.

1st Chain. As previous chs. RW.
1st Ring. As previous rs, joining 2nd p to 1st p of end ch, cl. RW.
2nd Chain. 4ds, p, 4ds, p, 4ds. RW.
2nd Ring. As previous r, joining to 2nd p of top ch, cl. RW.
3rd Chain. As previous ch. RW.
3rd Ring. As previous r, joining to 3rd p of top ch, cl. RW.
4th Chain. As 1st ch. DO NOT REVERSE WORK.

Ring. As first r of outer row.
Repeat to end working 2nd end to match 1st end. Fasten last ch to base of 1st r. Cut threads, tie, and overcast neatly. Press with a damp cloth and warm iron.

The backing can be made with ready-made frilling and ribbon stitched to the ends to tie, or with a pleated length of double silk or nylon, with the ends left long enough to tie.

NAPKIN RING

Work as for the Cake Frill, but join each row to form a circle.

Luncheon Mat of Motifs

Materials: Coats Mercer-Crochet No. 10 and 20. 2 balls ecru 610 in No. 10. 1 ball ecru 610 in No. 20. Tatting shuttle.

Measurements: 17″ × 11″, or any other size could be made.

One of the strongest and most beautiful of mats.

The medallions are made in shuttle thread only, and the filling between the medallions is worked with needle and cotton in No. 20.

1st MOTIF

1st Ring. 5ds, 6ps sep by 2ds, 5ds, cl.

2nd Ring. 5ds, join to last p of previous r, 2ds, 5ps sep by 2ds, 5ds, cl.

3rd Ring. As previous r.

4th Ring. 5ds, join to last p of previous r, 2ds, 4 ps sep by 2ds, 2ds, join to 1st p of 1st r, 5ds, cl.

Cut thread, tie to base of 1st r and overcast neatly.

2nd MOTIF

1st Ring. 5ds, 2 ps sep by 2ds, 2ds, join to 2nd free p of any r on previous motif, 2ds, join to next p of same r, 2ds, p, 2ds, p, 5ds, cl. Complete motif as first motif.

Join all motifs in this manner until the desired size is obtained.

Filling between motifs.

Thread needle with length of cotton. Pick up a p and cross to a p on the opposite side, giving the cotton a twist as it crosses. Continue until all the ps are joined. Securely fasten the threads in the centre and with the head of the needle, work backwards over one stitch and under two for three rounds. Fasten off on the back. Press with a damp cloth and warm iron.

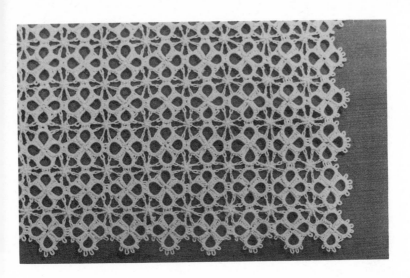

Attractive edging for Place Mat

Materials: Coats Mercer-Crochet No. 10. 3 balls ecru 610. Piece of heavy linen approx 22″ × 17″. Tatting shuttle.

Measurements of finished cloth: 22″ × 16½″. Depth of tatting 1¾″. Size of cloth after hemstitching 18″ × 13″. Fill shuttle with cotton but do not cut off from the ball.

1st Ring. *3ds, 7ps sep by 3ds, 3ds, cl. RW.

1st Chain. 5ds, 2ps sep by 3ds, 5ds. RW.

2nd Ring. 3ds, p, 3ds join to 6th p of previous r, 3ds, 5ps sep by 3ds, 3ds, cl. RW.

2nd Chain. 3ds, 16ps sep by 3ds, 3ds. RW.

3rd Ring. As 1st r, joining 4th p to 4th p of 2nd r, cl. RW.

3rd Chain. As 1st ch. RW.

4th Ring. As 2nd r, joining 4th p to 4th p of 1st r, cl. RW.

4th Chain. 3ds, p, 3ds. RW.

5th Ring. 3ds, p, 3ds, join to 6th p of 4th r, 3ds, 3ps sep by 3ds, 3ds, cl.

6th Ring. 3ds, join to last p of previous r, 3ds, 4ps sep by 3ds, 3ds, cl.

7th Ring. As 6th r. RW.

5th Chain. As 4th ch.

Repeat from beginning until 1st corner is reached (13 times for long side).

CORNER (after 5th ch)

1st Ring. 3ds, p, 3ds, join to 4th p of 7th r, 3ds, 5ps sep by 3ds, 3ds, cl. RW.

1st Chain. 5ds, join to 2nd p of 3rd

54

ch, 3ds, join to next p of same ch, 5ds, p, 5ds, p, 3ds, p, 5ds. RW.

2nd Ring. 3ds, 3ps sep by 3ds, join to centre p of 1st r, 3ds, 3ps sep by 3ds, 3ds, cl. RW.

2nd Chain. 3ds, p, 3ds, RW.

Corner is now made. Work as before, making 11 patterns to next corner. On last corner join last 2ps of large ch to ps of 1st ch and last r of clover to 1st r. Join last ch to base of 1st r. Hemstitch cloth with ¾" hem. Press. Stitch tatting to cloth with the 10 picots of long chain. Press with damp cloth and warm iron.

Gay Place Mat or Occasional Mat

Materials: Coats Mercer-Crochet No. 20. 3 balls orange 538, but any other shade may be used. Tatting shuttle.

Size of motif: $1\frac{3}{8}''$
Size of mat: $14\frac{1}{2}'' \times 11\frac{1}{2}''$

1st MOTIF
1st Ring. 10ds, 3ps sep by 4ds, 10 ds, cl.
2nd Ring. *10ds, join to last p of previous r, 4ds, 2ps sep by 4ds, 10ds, cl. Repeat from * 10 times more, joining last p of last r to 1st p of 1st r. Cut thread, tie securely to base of 1st r, oversew neatly.

2nd MOTIF
1st Ring. 10ds, p, 4ds, join to centre p of any r on 1st motif, 4ds, p, 10ds, cl.
2nd Ring. 10ds, join to last p of previous r, 4ds, join to p of next r on 1st motif, 4ds, p, 10ds, cl.
Complete as for 1st motif.
Work 7 rows of 9 motifs, joining

adjacent sides as 2nd motif was joined to 1st motif, leaving 1 free p between joins.

BORDER
1st ROW
With ball and shuttle thread.

1st Chain. Attach threads to free p to right of centre free p of any corner. *3ds, 2ps sep by 3ds, 3ds, join by shuttle thread to next p.

2nd Chain. 4ds, 5ps sep by 4ds, 4ds, join by shuttle thread to 2nd free p on next motif.

Repeat from * to next corner motif.
Chain. 3ds, 2ps sep by 3ds, 3ds, join by shuttle thread to next p.
Chain. 4ds, 5ps sep by 4ds, 4ds, miss 1 p join by shuttle thread to next p.

Repeat from 1st * joining last ch to same place as 1st ch.
Cut threads, tie, and oversew neatly.

2nd ROW
1st Ring. (As 1st r of 1st motif) 5 times, joining as before.

1st Chain. 3ds, 2ps sep by 3ds, 4ds, join by shuttle thread to 5th p of 2nd ch of previous row.

2nd Chain. *4ds, 2ps sep by 3ds, 3ds, join to last p of previous r, 3ds, 4ps sep by 3ds, 4ds, miss 2ps on previous row, join by shuttle thread to next p.

3rd Chain. 4ds, 2ps sep by 3ds, 3ds.
Ring. **10ds, join to 3rd p of 2nd last ch, 4ds, 2ps sep by 4ds, 10ds, cl. Work 4 more rs as for first motif.

4th Chain. 3ds, 2ps sep by 3ds, 4ds, miss 3ps on previous row, join by shuttle thread to next p.

Repeat from * to next corner, but only miss 1p on corner ch at end of last repeat.

Chain. 4ds, 2ps sep by 3ds, 3ds.
Ring. 10ds, join to last p of previous r, 4ds, 2ps sep by 4ds, 10ds, cl. Work 4 more rs as for 1st motif.

Chain. 3ds, 2ps sep by 3ds, 4ds, miss 1 p on previous row, join by shuttle thread to next p.

Repeat from 1st * ending last repeat at ** joining 2nd last ch to 1st p of 1st r and last ch to base of same r. Cut threads, tie and oversew neatly. Pin out to shape and size and press with a damp cloth and warm iron.

Luncheon Mat in two colours

Materials: Coats Mercer-Crochet No. 20. 2 balls 463 (Parrot Green) and 1 ball white, but any other two shades may be used. Tatting shuttle.

Measurements: 15" × 12".
First Strip. With green on shuttle,

1st ROW
1st Ring. (10ds, 3ps, sep by 2ds, 10ds, cl. RW) twice.
*Make a loop over base of rs, insert shuttle and pull tightly, space of ⅜".
3rd Ring. (5ds, join to last p of adjacent r, 5ds, 3ps sep by 2ds, 10ds, cl. RW) twice.
Repeat from * 33 times more, or until length required.

58

Cut thread, tie to base of last rs, overcast neatly.

2nd ROW
White only in ball and shuttle. Attach threads to base of first pair of rs worked, and weave in ends.
1st Chain. 12ds, p, 8ds, join by shuttle thread to 1st p on 1st r worked.
2nd Chain. * 5ds, p, 5ds, miss next p, join by shuttle thread to 1st free p on next r.
Repeat from * to next corner.
Chain. 5ds, p, 5ds, miss next p, join by shuttle thread to next p on same r.
Chain. 10ds, join by shuttle thread to 1st p on next r. Complete remaining side of strip to correspond. Cut threads, tie and overcast neatly.

Second Strip

Work as for 1st strip, joining each p on 1st side of 2nd row to corresponding p on 2nd side of first strip. Work 10 more strips, or more if required, joining as 2nd strip was joined to 1st strip.

Pin out, and press with damp cloth and warm iron.

Occasional or Place Mat

Materials: Coats Mercer-Crochet No. 20. 2 balls ecru No. 610. Tatting shuttle.

Medallion is approx. 2¼″ square. This mat is very suitable for Occasional Mat, Tray Mat, or Place Mat.

SQUARE MEDALLION
Centre Ring. 2ds, 8p, sep by 3ds, 1ds, cl. Cut threads, tie, and overcast neatly.
1st Ring. 3ds, p, 3ds, p, 3ds, join to any p of centre r, 3ds, p, 3ds, p, 3ds, cl. RW.
1st Chain. *3ds, 3p sep by 3ds, 3ds. RW.
2nd Ring. 3ds, p, 3ds, join to 2nd last p of last r, 3ds, join to next p of centre r, 3ds, p, 3ds, p, 3ds, cl. RW.
2nd Chain. 6ds, 4ps, sep by 6ds, 6ds. RW.
3rd Ring. As last r. RW.

Repeat from * joining last r to 1st r and last ch to top of 1st r. Cut threads, tie and oversew neatly.

Outer Round
1st Ring. *3ds, p, 3ds, p, 3ds, join to 1st p of a corner ch of centre section, 4ds, p, 4ds, cl. RW.
1st Chain. 5ds, p, 5ds, RW.
2nd Ring. 4ds, join to p of last r, 4ds, join to next p of corner ch, 3ds, p, 3ds, p, 3ds, cl. RW.
2nd Chain. 5ds, 4ps sep by 5ds, 5ds, RW.
3rd Ring. As 1st r, joining to 3rd p of corner ch. RW.
3rd Chain. 5ds, p, 5ds. RW.
4th Ring. As 2nd r. RW.
4th Chain. 5ds, p, 5ds, p, 5ds. RW.
Repeat from * 3 times, join last ch to top of 1st r. Cut threads, tie, overcast neatly.
Work 2nd medallion until 3rd

corner ch has been reached, proceed as follows:

Chain. 5ds, p, 5ds, p, 5ds, join to 3rd p of right hand corner ch of previous medallion, 5ds, join to last p of same ch, 5ds. RW.

Ring. As before.

Chain. 5ds, join to p of corresponding ch of previous medallion, 5ds. RW.

Ring. As before.

Chain. 5ds, join to 1st p of next ch, 5ds, join to 2nd p of same ch, 5ds. RW.

Ring. As before.

Chain. 5ds, join to p of next small ch of previous medallion, 5ds. RW.

Ring. As before.

Chain. 5ds, join to p of next ch of previous medallion, 5ds, join to next p of same ch, 5ds, p, 5ds, p, 5ds. RW.

Ring. As before. Complete medallion, joining last ch to top of 1st r. Cut threads, tie and overcast neatly.

Continue joining medallions until the required size is obtained.

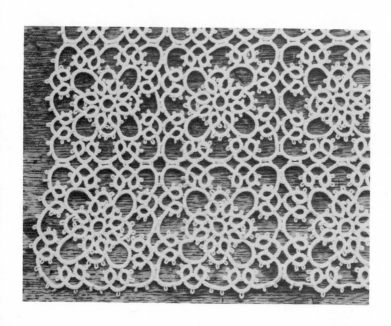

Place Mat in two colours

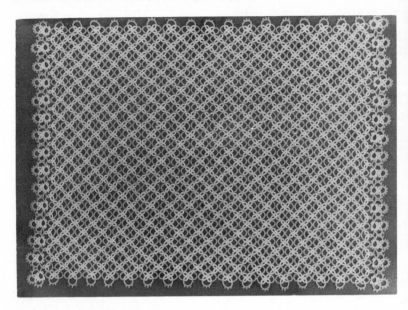

Materials: Coats Mercer-Crochet No. 20. 2 balls blue No. 680. 1 ball cherry No. 439, but any other two shades may be used. Tatting shuttle.

Measurements: $15\frac{1}{2}'' \times 11\frac{1}{2}''$.
Suitable for Place Mat or Occasional Table Mat.
Fill shuttle with blue cotton—cherry cotton in ball.
1st Ring. 6ds, p, 6ds, cl. RW.
2nd Ring. 6ds, p, 6ds, cl. RW.
1st chain. 6ds, p, 6ds. RW.
3rd Ring. *6ds, join to p of 2nd r, 6ds, cl. RW.
4th Ring. As 2nd r, cl. RW.
2nd Chain. 6ds, p, 6ds. RW.
Repeat from * until length required, joining 5th r to 4th r, cl. RW.
Turning ch at end of row, after joining of 5th r to 4th r.

Chain. 6ds, 3ps sep by 3ds, 6ds. RW.
Ring. 6ds, join to same p as previous 2 rs, 6ds, cl. RW.

Continue as before, joining rs to form groups of 4, and joining ps of ch to adjacent ps of ch of previous row. Repeat to end of row, and work turning ch to match 1st end.
Cut cotton, tie, and overcast neatly. Repeat these two rows, joining as before, until required length.

EDGING
1st Ring. * 2ds, p, 2ds, p, 2ds, join to centre p of 1st ch of end row, 2ds 8ps, sep by 2ds, 2ds, cl. RW.
1st Chain. 4ds, 3ps sep by 3ds, 3ds. RW.
2nd Ring. 5ds, join to 3rd p of 1st r, 5ds, cl. RW.

62

2nd Chain. 2ds, 6ps sep by 2ds, 2ds. RW.

3rd Ring. 5ds, join to same p as previous r, 5ds, cl. RW.

3rd Chain. 3ds, p, 3ds, p, 3ds, 1 long p, 4ds, Join to 6th p of 1st r, 4ds. RW.

4th Ring. 6ds, join to p between two rs of first row, cl. RW.

4th Chain. 4ds. RW.

Repeat from * joining 1st p of 1st ch to long p of 3rd ch.

Repeat for length of mat finishing with 3rd ch, and small p instead of long p.

Work second side to match.

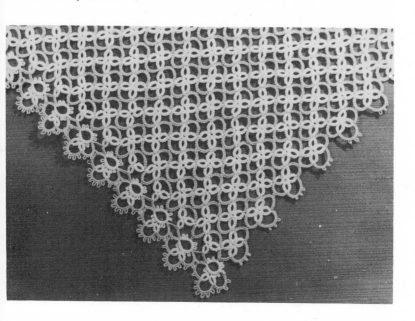

Dainty Occasional Mat

Materials: Coats Mercer-Crochet No. 20. 2 balls 8906 (multi-colour). Tatting shuttle.

Measurements: Centre Mat, 12½″ diameter.

CENTRE MAT
Centre Medallion

1st ROW
R of 1ds, 8ps sep by 2ds, 1ds, cl. Tie securely and without cutting thread, join to 1st p of r.

2nd ROW
1st Ring. 4ds, p, 12ds, p, 12ds, p, 4ds, cl, join to 2nd p of centre.
2nd Ring. *4ds, join to last p of previous r, 12ds, p, 12ds, p, 4ds, cl, join to next p of centre.
Repeat from * 6 times more, joining last p of last r to 1st p of 1st r.
Cut threads and tie to base of first p of centre, overcast ends neatly.

3rd ROW
1st Ring. 3ds, p, 3ds, join to centre p of any r of centre medallion, 3ds, p, 3ds, cl. RW. leave ⅛″ length of thread.
2nd Ring. 4ds, 3ps sep by 4ds, 4ds, cl. RW. leave ⅛″ length of thread.
3rd Ring. 3ds, join to last p of previous small r, 3ds, p, 3ds, p, 3ds, cl. RW; leave ⅛″ length of thread.
4th Ring. 4ds, join to last p of previous r, 4ds, p, 4ds, p, 4ds, cl, RW; leave ⅛″ length of thread.
Repeat last 2 rs once more.

64

Join centre p of next small r to centre p of next r of previous row.

Repeat all around centre medallion, joining last p of last small r to first p of 1st small r, and last p of last r to first p of 1st r (24 small rs and 24 rs) leave $\frac{1}{8}''$ length of thread, cut thread and join to base of 1st r, tie, overcast neatly.

4th ROW

Make medallion as before, joining centre p of 1st and 2nd r to centre p of 1st and 3rd r on 3rd row. Make another medallion, joining 1st and 2nd r to centre p of 4th and 6th r of 3rd row, and centre p of last r to centre p of 3rd r on previous medallion. Make 6 more medallions, joining each as before, always leaving 1 free r between joinings of rs and joining 1 petal of last medallion to petal of first medallion.

5th ROW

As 3rd row, joining 2 small rs to centre p of 2 petals on medallion, leaving one small r free between petals and 6 small rs free between medallions (one free petal left on each side of each medallion).

6th ROW

Work 18 medallions as before, joining centre p of 2 petals, to centre p of 2 rs on 5th row, leaving one r free between joinings, and joining one petal of each medallion to one petal of adjacent medallion.

7th ROW

As 3rd row, joining 2 small rs to centre p of 2 petals on medallion, leaving one small r free between petals and 4 small rs free between medallion.

SCALLOPED EDGE

1st Ring. 3ds, p, 2ds, join to centre p of r on previous row, 2ds, 5ps sep by 2ds, 3ds, cl. RW.

1st Chain. *3ds 7ps sep by 2ds, 3ds. RW.

2nd Ring. 3ds, p, 2ds, join to second last p of previous r, 2ds, 5ps, sep by 2ds, 3ds, cl. RW.

Repeat from * 4 times more.

6th Chain. 3ds, 7ps sep by 2ds, 3ds. RW.

7th Ring. *3ds, p, 2ds, join to 2nd last p of previous r, 2ds, 3ps, sep by 2ds, 2ds, miss 4 rs of previous row, join to centre p of next r, 2ds, p, 3ds. cl. Do not RW.

7th Chain. 5ds, join to centre p of next r, 5ds. Do not RW.

1st Ring. As previous 1st r, joining to next p of previous row.

Repeat from * joining 2nd p of 1st ch to 6th p of 6th ch.

Repeat all around mat.

On last repeat join 6th p of 6th ch to 2nd p of 1st ch and ending with, RW. r of 3ds, p, 2ds, join to 2nd last p of previous r, 2ds, 3ps sep by 2ds, 2ds, miss 4 rs of previous row, join to centre p of next r of previous row, 2ds, p, 3ds, cl. Do not RW.

Chain of 5ds, join to centre p of next r of previous row, 5ds. Join to base of 1st r, Cut threads, tie and overcast neatly.

Occasional Mat

Materials: Coats Mercer-Crochet No. 20. 2 balls spec. 8906. Tatting shuttle.

Measurement: $12'' \times 9\frac{1}{2}''$.

Centre. Fill shuttle with cotton but do not cut it off from the ball.

1st Ring. *5ds, p, 5ds, long p ($\frac{1}{4}''$), 5ds, p, 5ds, cl. RW.

1st Chain. 3ds, 7ps sep by 3ds, 3ds. RW.

2nd Ring. 5ds, p, 5ds, join to long p, 5ds, p, 5ds. cl.

Repeat from * twice more.

4th Chain. As before.

7th Ring. **5ds, p, 5ds, join to last long p, 5ds, p, 5ds, cl. RW.

5th Chain. As before.

8th Ring. 5ds, p, 5ds, join to same long p, 5ds, p, 5ds. cl.

Repeat from ** twice more joining to each of next 2 long ps, in turn.

8th Chain. As before, join to base of 1st r.

Cut threads, tie and overcast neatly.

1st Round

1st Ring. *5ds, p, 5ds, join to 6th p of last ch of centre, 5ds, p, 5ds, cl. RW.

1st Chain. 3ds, 5 ps sep by 3ds, 3ds. RW.

2nd Ring. 5ds, p, 5ds, join to 4th p of same ch, 5ds, p, 5ds, cl. RW.

2nd Chain. As before.

3rd Ring. 5ds, p, 5ds, join to 2nd p of same ch, 5ds, p, 5ds, cl. RW.

3rd Chain. As before.

4th Ring. As before joining to 5th p of next ch.

67

4th Chain. As before.
5th Ring. As before, joining to 3rd p of same ch.
5th Chain. As before.
Repeat the last two rs and chs twice more.
Repeat from * once more.
Cut threads, tie and overcast neatly.

2nd Round

1st Ring. *(5ds, p, 5ds, long p, 5ds, p, 5ds, cl. RW.
1st Chain. 3ds, 3ps sep by 3ds, 3ds, join to centre p of 4th ch of previous round, 3ds, 3ps sep by 3ds, 3ds. RW.
2nd Ring. 5ds p, 5ds, join to last long p, 5ds, p, 5ds, cl.) 5 times.
Ring. (5ds, p, 5ds, long p, 5ds, p, 5ds, cl. RW.
Chain. 3ds, 3ps sep by 3ds, join to 2nd p of next ch, 3ds, 3ps sep by 3ds, 3ds. RW.
Ring. 5ds, p, 5ds, join to last long p, 5ds, p, 5ds, cl.
Ring. As before.
Chain. As before, joining to 4th p of same ch.
Ring. As before), 4 times.
Repeat from * once more.
Cut threads, tie and overcast neatly.

3rd Round

1st Ring. *5ds, p, 5ds, join to any long p of previous round, 5ds, p, 5ds, cl. RW.
1st Chain. 3ds, 7ps sep by 3ds, 3ds. RW.
2nd Ring. 5ds, p, 5ds, join to same long p as previous r, 5ds, p, 5ds, cl.
Repeat from * all round.
Cut threads, tie and overcast neatly.

4th Round

1st Ring. *5ds, p, 5ds, join to 5th p of any ch of previous round, 5ds, p, 5ds, cl. RW.

1st Chain. 3ds, 3ps sep by 3ds, 3ds. RW.
2nd Ring. 5ds, p, 5ds, join to 3rd p of same ch, 5ds, p, 5ds, cl. RW.
2nd Chain. As before.
Repeat from * all round.
Cut threads, tie and overcast neatly.

5th Round

Mark ch immediately above centre r joined to end ch of centre. Join thread to centre p of this ch.
1st Chain. *3ds, 5ps sep by 3ds, 3ds, join to centre p of next ch.
2nd Chain. (3ds, 3ps sep by 3ds, 3ds, join to centre p of next ch) 24 times.
26th Chain. 3ds, 5ps sep by 3ds, 3ds, join to centre p of next ch.
Repeat from * once more.
Cut threads, tie to same p as 1st r was joined, overcast neatly.

6th Round* 1st Motif

1st Ring. 3ds, 7ps sep by 3ds, 3ds, cl.
2nd Ring. 3ds, join to last p of previous r, 3ds, 8 ps sep by 3ds, 3ds, cl.
3rd Ring. 3ds, join to last p of previous r, 3ds, 6ps sep by 3ds, 3ds, cl. RW.
1st Chain. 6ds, 3ps sep by 3ds, 3ds, join to centre p of last ch of round 5, 3ds, p, 3ds. RW.
4th Ring. **3ds, p, 3ds, join to 3rd free p of adjacent r of trefoil, 3ds, p, 3ds, cl. RW.
2nd Chain. 3ds, 3ps sep by 3ds, 3ds. RW.
Repeat from ** 9 times more, joining each r in turn to next p of 1st r, to centre 5ps of centre r and to 2nd and 3rd free ps of 3rd r.
Ring. As before, joining to next p of same r.
Chain. 3ds, p, 3ds, join to centre p of 1st ch of round 5, 3ds, p, 3ds,

p, 3ds, join to 1st p of 1st ch of motif, 6ds, join to base of trefoil. Cut threads, tie and overcast neatly.

2nd Motif

Work trefoil as for 1st motif.
1st Chain. 6ds, 3ps sep by 3ds, 3ds, join to centre p of 2nd ch of round 5, 3ds, p, 3ds. RW.
Continue as for 1st motif, joining 2nd p of 2nd and 3rd chs to corresponding ps of 1st motif as far as end of last small r.

Chain. 3ds, p, 3ds, join to centre p of 4th ch of round 5, 3ds, 2ps sep by 3ds, 3ds, join to 1st p of 1st ch, 6ds, join to base of trefoil.

Cut threads, tie and overcast neatly.
Work 7 more motifs as 2nd motif, joining to 5th and 7th, 8th and 10th chs, etc.
Repeat from * once more, joining last motif to 1st to complete round.
Pin out to shape and press with a damp cloth and warm iron.

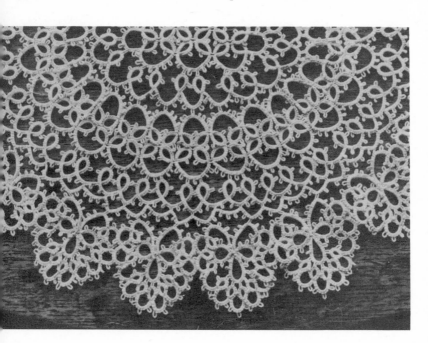

Round Mat

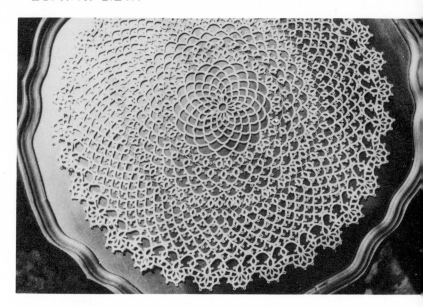

Materials: Coats Mercer-Crochet No. 20. 2 balls pale pink 624. Tatting shuttle. Strip of thin card $\frac{3}{8}''$ wide.

Measurement: 13″ diameter.

A lovely delicate tatted mat with a pretty shell edge.

Centre Ring. Working long ps over strip of card, 1ds, 16 long ps sep by 2ds, 1 ds, cl; cut threads, tie and overcast neatly.

1st Round. Join both threads to any p of previous r, as described in the instructions at the beginning of this book. (page 21)

Chain. *3ds, p, 3ds, join to next p, repeat from * to end, cut and tie and overcast neatly.

2nd Round. Join to a p of previous round.

Chain. *4ds, p, 4ds, join to p of next ch, repeat from * to end, cut, tie and overcast neatly.

3rd Round. As 2nd, but work 5ds, p, 5ds in each ch.

4th Round. As 2nd, but work 6ds, p, 6ds in each ch.

5th Round. As 2nd, but work 7ds, p, 7ds, in each ch.

6th Round. As 2nd, but work 8ds, p, 8ds in each ch.

7th Round. Join threads to p of previous round, *3ds, 5ps, sep by 3ds, 3ds, join to p of next ch. Repeat from * to end, cut and tie and overcast neatly.

8th Round.

1st Ring. *4ds, 3ps sep by 4ds, 4ds, cl. RW. Leave $\frac{1}{4}''$ thread between all rs.

2nd Ring. 4ds, p, 4ds, join to 4th p of ch of round 7, 4ds, p, 4ds, cl. RW.

3rd Ring. As 1st r. RW.

4th Ring. As 2nd r, joining to 2nd p of same ch. Repeat from * to end, cut and tie and overcast neatly.

9th Round. Join to centre p of any r on outer row of round 8.

Chain. *3ds, 3ps, sep by 3ds, 3ds, join to centre p of next r. Repeat from * to end, cut and tie and overcast neatly.

10th Round. Join to centre p of any ch of round 9.

Chain. *4ds, 3ps sep by 3ds, 4ds, join to centre p of next ch. Repeat from * to end, cut and tie and overcast neatly.

11th Round. Join to centre p of ch of round 10.

Chain. *3ds, 5ps sep by 3ds, 3ds, join to centre p of next ch. Repeat from * to end, cut and tie and overcast neatly.

12th Round. As 8th round.

13th Round. As 9th round.

14th Round. Join to centre p of ch of round 13.

Chain. *3ds, 3ps, sep by 3ds, 3ds, join to centre p of next ch. Repeat from * to end. Cut and tie and overcast neatly.

15th Round. As 14th round.

16th Round. As 10th round.

17th Round. As 10th round.

18th Round.

1st Ring. *4ds, p, 4ds, 6 long ps over card, sep by 1ds, 4ds, p, 4ds, cl. RW.

1st Chain. 4ds, p, 4ds, join to centre p of ch of round 17, 4ds, p, 4ds. RW.

2nd Ring. 4ds, 3ps, sep by 4ds, 4ds, cl. RW.

2nd Chain. 4ds, p, 4ds, join to centre p of next ch, 4ds, p, 4ds. RW. Repeat from * to end, cut and tie and overcast neatly.

19th Round. Join thread to centre p of small ring *(3ds, p, 3ds, join to next long p) 6 times, 3ds, p, 3ds; join to centre p of next small r. Repeat from * to end, cut and tie and overcast neatly.

20th Round.

1st Ring. *4ds, join to p of ch on right of small r, 4ds, join to p of ch on left of small r, 4ds, cl. RW.

1st Chain. 3ds, join to p of next ch, (3ds, p, 3ds, join to p of next ch) 4 times, 3ds.

Repeat from * to end. Cut threads, tie and overcast neatly.

Motif Mat with Scalloped Border

Materials: Coats Mercer-Crochet Cotton No. 20. 2 balls ecru 610, but any other colour may be used. Tatting shuttle.

Measurement: 12½″ square. 16 medallions.

MEDALLION
Four-leaf Clover
1st Ring. 3ds, 13ps sep by 3ds, 3ds, cl.
2nd Ring. 3ds, join to last p of last r, 3ds, 12ps sep by 3ds, 3ds, cl.
3rd Ring. As previous r.
4th Ring. 3ds, join to last p of previous r, 3ds, 11ps sep by 3ds, 3ds, join to 1st p of 1st r, 3ds. Close. Cut threads, tie to base of 1st r, oversew neatly.

BORDER OF MEDALLION
1st Ring. 3ds, 5ps sep by 3ds, 3ds, cl.
2nd Ring. *Close beside 1st r, 3ds, 5ps sep by 3ds, 3ds, cl. RW.
1st Chain. 5ds, p, 5ds, p, 5ds. RW.
3rd Ring. 5ds, join to 3rd p of last r, 5ds, join to 6th p of a r of 4-leaf clover, 5ds, p, 5ds, cl. RW.
2nd Chain. As 1st ch. RW.
4th Ring. 3ds, p, 3ds, p, 3ds, join to p of last r, 3ds, p, 3ds, p, 3ds, cl.
5th Ring. Close beside 4th r, 3ds, 5ps sep by 3ds, 3ds, cl. RW.
3rd Chain. 5ds, p, 5ds, 5ps sep by 3ds, 5ds, p, 5ds. RW.
6th Ring. 3ds, p, 3ds, p, 3ds, join to 3rd p of last r, 3ds, p, 3ds, p, 3ds, cl.
Repeat from * all round, joining last pair of rs to 1st pair.

Join last corner ch between 1st pair of rs.

Cut threads, tie and oversew neatly.

To join medallions.

Work next medallion as above until 2nd pair of rs have been made, then work corner ch thus:

5ds, p, 5ds, 4ps sep by 3ds, 3ds, join to 5th p of group of 5 p on lower right corner ch of last medallion, 5ds, join to next p of same ch of last medallion, 5ds. RW.

Next pair of rs as in last medallion. RW.

Chain. 5ds, join to 1st p of next ch of last medallion, 5ds, join to 2nd p of same chain, 5ds. RW.

Ring. As in last medallion. RW.

Chain. As last. RW.

Ring. Pair of rs as before. RW.

Chain. 5ds, join to 1st p of next ch of last medallion, 5ds, join to 2nd p of same ch, 3ds, 4ps sep by 3ds, 5ds, p, 5ds.

Complete medallion as before.

When joining the 4th medallion to form a square, join along the 1st side as directed, then when working the 2nd corner ch join it to 1st and 2nd ps of corner ch of medallion on left, then work 3ds, 3ps sep by 3ds, 3ds, join to 5th p of the group of 5 ps of lower left corner ch of medallion above on right, 5ds, join to last p of that ch, 5ds.

Make joins to next 3 chs as before, and complete medallion.

Row of rings and chains.

1st Ring. 6ds, 3ps sep by 6ds, 6ds, cl. RW.

1st Chain. *5ds, join to 1st p of right-hand corner ch of a medallion (but not at right-hand corner of mat), 5ds, join to 2nd p of same ch, 5ds. RW.

2nd Ring. 6ds, join to last p of last r, 6ds, p, 6ds, p, 6ds, cl. RW.

2nd Chain. 5ds, join to 4th p of same ch of medallion, 5ds. RW.

3rd Ring. As last r. RW.

3rd Chain. 5ds, join to 2nd p of 1st ch of next medallion, 5ds. RW.

4th Ring. As last. RW.

4th Chain. 5ds, join to last p of group of ps on same ch, 5ds, join to last p of same ch, 5ds. RW.

5th Ring. As last. RW.

5th Chain. 5ds, join to 1st p of next ch, 5ds, join to 2nd p of same ch, 5ds. RW.

6th Ring. As last. RW.

6th Chain. As last ch. RW.

7th Ring. As last. RW.

Repeat from * until a ch has been joined to 1st 2ps of outer corner ch of end medallion.

Ring. As last. RW.

Chain. 5ds, join to 4th p of corner ch, 7ds. RW.

CLOVER LEAF

1st Ring. As last r.

2nd Ring. 6ds, join to last p of last r, 6ds, 3ps sep by 6ds, 6ds, cl.

3rd Ring. 6ds, join to last p of last r, 6ds, p, 6ds, p, 6ds, cl. RW.

Chain. 7ds, join to same p as last ch, 5ds. RW.

Ring. As last, and continue as before right round, taking care to make rings and chains consecutive at end of round.

EDGING SCALLOPS

First work centre rings for corner scallops.

CORNER RINGS

2ds, 4ps sep by 3ds, 3ds, join to 1st p of 2nd r of a corner clover of last round, 6ds, join to 2nd p of same r, 3ds, 4ps sep by 3ds, 1ds, cl.

Cut thread, tie and oversew neatly.

Work three more similarly for the other corners.

Now work the corner scallops.

Join thread to p of 1st r of corner clover.

1st Ring. 3ds, p, 3ds, p, 3ds, join to lowest p of centre r, 3ds, p, 3ds, p, 3ds, cl. RW.

1st Chain. 3ds, 3ps sep by 3ds, 3ds. RW.

2nd Ring. 3ds, p, 3ds, join to 2nd last p of last r, 3ds, join to next p of centre r, 3ds, p, 3ds, p, 3ds, cl. RW.

2nd Chain. 3ds, 4ps sep by 3ds, 3ds. RW.

Work 3 more similar rs with 3 chs of 3ds, 5ps sep by 3ds, 3ds.

After 6th r has been joined to centre r, make a chain of 3ds, 4ps sep by 3ds. RW.

7th Ring. As last RW.

7th Chain. 3ds, 3ps sep by 3ds, 3ds, RW.

8th Ring. As last. Close and join to p of 3rd r of clover. Cut threads, tie and oversew neatly.

Work three more corners in the same way.

Centre rings for scallops each side of corner scallops.

Ring. 2ds, 3ps sep by 3ds, 3ds, join to 2nd p of last round on right of corner scallop, 3ds, 3ps sep by 3ds, 1ds, cl.

Cut threads, tie and oversew neatly. Turn work over and join a smilar r to 2nd r to other side of scallop. Work two rs beside other 3 corner scallops.

Remainder of Border

Join a similar r to 4th r in last row from last centre r, and to every 4th r along all sides of the work.

Join thread to p of 1st r of last round on right of corner scallop.

1st Ring. *As 1st r of corner scallop. RW.

1st Chain. 3ds, p, 3ds, join to 2nd p of last ch of last scallop, 3ds, p, 3ds. RW.

2nd Ring. As in other scallops. RW.
2nd Chain. 3ds, 4ps sep by 3ds, 3ds. RW.
3rd Ring. As last. RW.
3rd Chain. 3ds, 5ps sep by 3ds, 3ds. RW.
4th Ring. As last. RW.
4th Chain. As 2nd ch. RW.
5th Ring. As last. RW.
5th Chain. 3ds, 3ps sep by 3ds, 3ds. RW.
6th Ring. As last, cl and join to p of next r of last round. DO NOT REVERSE.
6th Chain. 6ds, join to p of next r of last round. RW.

7th Ring. 6ds, join to centre p of adjacent ch, 6ds, p, 6ds, p, 6ds, cl. RW.
7th Chain. 6ds, join to p of next r of last round. DO NOT REVERSE.
Repeat from * joining centre p of 1st ch of next scallop, to adjacent p of large r.
Work along to next corner scallop, joining last p of last large r to centre p of 1st ch of corner scallop and last 6ds ch to base of 1st r.
Cut threads, tie and oversew neatly. Pin out to shape and press with a damp cloth and warm iron.

Dressing Table Mat

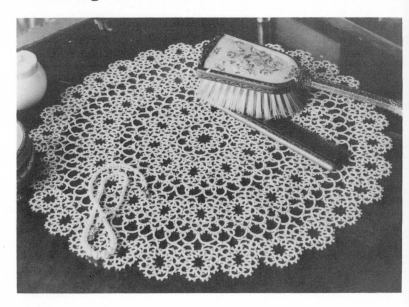

Materials: Coats Mercer-Crochet No. 20. 2 balls. This model is worked in shade 690 (mauve), but any other shade of cotton may be used. Tatting shuttle.

Measurement: 15½" diameter.

1st Round. Fill shuttle with cotton but do not cut it off from the ball.

1st Ring. 3ds, 5ps sep by 3ds, 3ds, cl. RW.

1st Chain. *3ds, 3ps sep by 3ds, 3ds. RW.

2nd Ring. 3ds, p, 3ds, join to 2nd last p on previous r, 3ds, 3ps sep by 3ds, 3ds, cl. RW.

Repeat from * 8 times more, joining 2nd last p of last r, to 2nd p on 1st r. Chain of 3ds, 3ps sep by 3ds, 3ds, join to base of 1st r.

Cut ends, tie and overcast neatly.

2nd Round. Join threads to centre p of any ch on previous row, weave in ends.

Chain. 4ds, p, *6ds, 2ps sep by 4ds, 6ds, **p, 4ds, join by shuttle thread to centre p of next ch on previous row, 4ds, join to last p on adjacent ch, repeat from * ending last repeat at **, join to 1st p on 1st ch, 4ds, join to same p as 1st ch was attached. Cut threads, tie and overcast neatly.

3rd Round.

1st Ring. 3ds, 5ps sep by 3ds, 3ds, cl. RW.

1st Chain. Join thread to top of r and weave in ends.

Ch of 6ds, join to 1st free p of ch on previous row, 3ds, p, 6ds. DO NOT REVERSE.

2nd Ring. †3ds, 5ps sep by 3ds, 3ds, cl. RW.

2nd Chain. 4ds, join to 2nd last p on adjacent r, 3ds, 2ps sep by 3ds, 4ds. RW.

3rd Ring. *(3ds, p, 3ds, join to 2nd last p on previous r, 3ds, 3ps, sep by 3ds, 3ds, cl. RW.†

3rd Chain. 4ds, 3ps sep by 3ds, 4ds. RW.) 7 times.

10th Ring. 3ds, p, 3ds, join to 2nd last p on previous r, 3ds, p, 3ds, join to 2nd p on adjacent r, 3ds, p, 3ds, cl. DO NOT REVERSE.

10th Chain. 6ds, join to p on adjacent ch, 3ds, join to next p of ch on previous row, 6ds. RW.

11th Ring. 3ds, p, 3ds, join to 1st p on adjacent ch, 3ds, 3ps sep by 3ds, 3ds, cl. RW.

11th Chain. 6ds, join to 1st p of next ch on previous row, 3ds, p, 6ds. DO NOT REVERSE.

Repeat within † † once.

Chain. 4ds, p, 3ds, join to corresponding p on adjacent ch, 3ds, p, 4ds. RW. ** repeat from * working within ( ) 6 times and ending last repeat at **.

Repeat within ( ) 4 times.

Ring. As before. RW.

Chain. 4ds, p, 3ds, join to corresponding p on adjacent ch, 3ds, p, 4ds. RW.

Ring. As before. RW.

Chain. 4ds, 2ps sep by 3ds, 3ds, join to second p of 1st r, 4ds. RW.

Ring. 3ds, p, 3ds, join to 2nd p on previous r, 3ds, p, 3ds, join to 2nd p on adjacent r, 3ds, p, 3ds, cl. RW.
Chain. 6ds, join to p on adjacent ch, 3ds, join to next p on previous row, 6ds, join to base of 1st r. Cut threads, tie and overcast neatly.

4th Round.

1st Ring. 2ds, 3ps sep by 3ds, 3ds, join to centre p of 6th 3 p chain on previous round. 4ds, p, 4ds, join to centre p on adjacent ch, 3ds, 3ps sep by 3ds, 2ds, cl. RW. Join thread to top of r and weave in ends.

1st Chain. *4ds, 6 ps sep by 2ds, 4ds, join by shuttle thread to centre p of next ch, 4ds, 5ps sep by 2ds, 4ds, join by shuttle thread to centre p on next ch, 4ds, 6ps sep by 2ds, 4ds. RW.

2nd Ring. **2ds, 3ps sep by 3ds, 3ds, join to centre p on next ch, 4ds, p, 4ds, join to centre p on next ch, 3ds, 3ps sep by 3ds, 2ds, cl. RW.

Repeat from * ending last repeat at **, join to base of first ring. Cut threads, tie and overcast neatly.

5th Round.

1st Ring. 8ds, join to last p of last ch on previous round, 3ds, join to 1st p on next ch, 8ds, cl. RW.

1st Chain. Join thread to top of r and weave in ends.

4ds, p, *7ds, p, 9ds, p, 4ds, miss 2ps on previous round, join by shuttle thread to next p, 4ds, join to corresponding p on adjacent ch, 9ds, p, 7ds, p, 4ds. RW.

2nd Ring. 8ds, miss 4ps on previous round, join to next p, 8ds, cl. RW.
2nd Chain. 4ds, join to corresponding p on adjacent ch, 7ds, p, 9ds, p, 4ds, miss 4ps on previous round join by shuttle thread to next p, 4ds, join to corresponding p on adjacent ch, 9ds, p, 7ds, **p, 4ds. RW.

3rd Ring. 8ds, miss 2ps, join to next p, 3ds, join to next p, 8ds, cl. RW.

3rd Chain. 4ds, join to corresponding p on adjacent ch.

Repeat from * ending last repeat at **, join to 1st p on 1st ch, 4ds, join to base of 1st r. Cut threads, tie and overcast neatly.

6th Round.

1st Ring. 2ds, 7ps sep by 3ds, 2ds,

cl. RW. Join thread and weave in ends.

1st Chain. 6ds, p, 3ds, join to free p of 1st ch on previous round, 3ds, p, 6ds.

2nd Ring. *3ds, 5ps sep by 3ds, 3ds, cl. RW.

2nd Chain. 4ds, 2ps sep by 3ds, 3ds, join to 3rd p of adjacent r, 4ds. RW.

3rd Ring. (3ds, p, 3ds, join to 2nd last p of last r, 3ds, 3ps sep by 3ds, 3ds, cl. RW.

3rd Chain. *4ds, 3ps sep by 3ds, 4ds. RW) 7 times.

10th Ring. **3ds, p, 3ds, join to 2nd last p of previous r, 3ds, p, 3ds, join to 2nd p of adjacent r, 3ds, p, 3ds, cl. DO NOT REVERSE.

10th Chain. 6ds, p, 3ds, join to p of next ch on previous round, 3ds, p, 6ds. RW.

11th Ring. 2ds, 2ps sep by 3ds, 3ds, join to 3rd p on adjacent ch, 3ds, 4ps sep by 3ds, 2ds, cl. RW.

11th Chain. 6ds, p, 3ds, join to p of next ch on previous round, 3ds, p, 6ds. DO NOT REVERSE.

Repeat from * to * once.

Chain. 4ds, p, 3ds, join to corresponding p of adjacent ch, 3ds, p, 4ds. RW.

***Repeat within ( ) 6 times.

Repeat from ** ending last repeat at ***.

Repeat within ( ) 4 times.

Ring. As before. RW.

Chain. 4ds, p, 3ds, join to corresponding p of adjacent ch, 3ds, p, 4ds. RW.

Ring. As before. RW.

Chain. 4ds, join to 2nd p of adjacent r, 3ds, 2ps sep by 3ds, 4ds. RW.

Ring. 3ds, p, 3ds, join to 2nd last p of previous r, 3ds, p, 3ds, join to 2nd p of adjacent r, 3ds, p, 3ds, cl. DO NOT REVERSE.

Chain. 6ds, p, 3ds, join to p of next ch on previous round, 3ds, p, 6ds, join to base of 1st r. Cut threads, tie and overcast neatly.

7th Round. As 4th round.

8th Round.

1st Ring. 8ds, miss 2ps on 1st ch on previous round, join to next p, 2ds, join to next p, 8ds, cl. RW.

1st Chain. Join thread and weave in ends.

*(10ds, p) twice, 4ds, miss 4ps on previous round, join by shuttle thread to next p, 4ds, join to corresponding p on adjacent ch (10ds, p, 10ds. RW.

2nd Ring. 8ds, miss 4ps on previous round, join to next p, 2ds, join to next p, 8ds cl. RW) twice.

Repeat from * omitting ring at end of last repeat, join to base of 1st r. Cut threads, tie and overcast neatly.

9th Round. As 6th Round.

Pin out carefully, and press over a damp cloth with a warm iron.

Collar in two colours

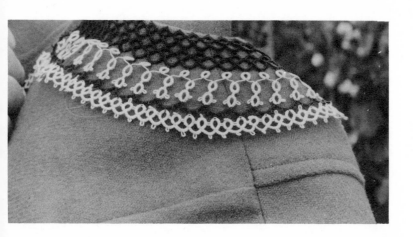

Materials: Coats Mercer-Crochet No. 40. 1 ball ecru 610. 1 ball dark brown 836. Tatting shuttle.

1st Row. With dark brown cotton, fill shuttle but do not cut it off from the ball.
1st Ring. 4ds, 3ps sep by 4ds, 4ds, cl. RW.
1st Chain. *6ds, p, 6ds, RW.
2nd Ring. 4ds, join to adjacent p of 1st r, 4ds, p, 4ds, p, 4ds, cl. RW.
Repeat from * to end.
Turning chain, DO NOT REVERSE, 1ds, p, 3ds, p, 6ds.
2nd Row.
1st Ring. 4ds, p, 4ds, join to p of 1st ch of last row, 4ds, p, 4ds, cl. RW.
1st Chain. *7ds, p, 7ds. R.W
2nd Ring. 4ds, join to adjacent p of 1st r, 4ds, join to p of 2nd ch of 1st

row, 4ds, p, 4ds, cl. RW.
Repeat from * to end, working 2nd turning ch to match 1st. Cut threads, tie and oversew neatly.
3rd Row. With ecru cotton and shuttle only:
1st Ring. *8ds, join to p of 1st ch of 2nd row, 8ds, cl. RW. Leave $\frac{1}{4}''$ length of thread.
2nd Ring. 8ds, p, 8ds, cl. RW. Leave $\frac{1}{4}''$ length of thread.
Repeat from * to end. Cut thread and oversew neatly.
4th Row. With ecru in shuttle and brown in ball:
1st Ring. *4ds, p, 4ds, join to p of 2nd r of previous row, 4ds, p, 4ds, cl. RW.
1st Chain. 4ds, 3ps sep by 4ds, 4ds. RW.
Repeat from * to end.

5th Row. With ecru in shuttle and ball:
1st Ring. *4ds, p, 4ds, join to centre p of 1st ch of previous row, 4ds, p, 4ds, cl. RW.
1st Chain. 4ds, p, 4ds, RW.
2nd Ring. 4ds, join to adjacent p of 1st r, 4ds, p, 4ds, p, 4ds, cl. RW.
2nd Chain. 4ds, p, 4ds. RW.

Repeat from * to end. Cut threads, tie and oversew neatly.
Press with damp cloth and warm iron. Stitch to dress by the ps of the rs of the 1st row.
Stitch again by the ps of the chs of the second row; this will keep the collar lying flat.

Collar with shell edging

Materials: Coats Mercer-Crochet No. 40. 1 ball beige 609. Tatting shuttle. Strip of thin card, $3'' \times \frac{3}{8}''$.

1st ROW
Fill shuttle with cotton but do not cut it off from the ball.
1st Ring. *4ds, p, 4ds, p, 4ds, p, 4ds, cl. RW.
1st Chain. 4ds, p, 4ds. RW.
2nd Ring. 4ds, join to last p of previous r, 4ds, p, 4ds, p, 4ds, cl. RW.
2nd Chain. As 1st ch.
Repeat from * for length required, finishing after a r.

Turn for 2nd row with a ch of 8ds, p, 8ds, p, 8ds. RW.

2nd ROW
1st Ring. *4ds, p, 4ds, join to centre p of last r of previous row, 4ds, p, 4ds, cl. RW.
1st Chain. 3ds, 3ps sep by 3ds, 3ds. RW.
2nd Ring. 4ds, p, 4ds, join to centre p of next r of previous row, 4ds, p, 4ds, cl. RW.
Repeat from * to end joining to 1st row by ch to match 1st end.

80

Cut threads, tie to base of r and oversew neatly.

3rd ROW
1st Chain. Join thread to base of 1st r of 2nd row, and weave in ends. 8ds, p, 8ds, p, 3ds, join by shuttle thread to centre p of 1st ch of 1st row.

2nd Chain. *3ds, 3ps sep by 3ds, 3ds, join by shuttle thread to centre p of next ch on 2nd row.

Repeat from * to end, finishing with ch to match 1st end and joining to the base of last r of previous row.

Cut threads, tie and oversew neatly.

4th ROW
1st Chain. Join threads to 2nd p of 1st ch of previous row, 4ds, p, 4ds, join by shuttle thread to centre p of next ch of previous row.

2nd Chain. 4ds, p, 3ds, p, 3ds, p, 4ds, join by shuttle thread to centre p of next ch of previous row.

Repeat to end, making last ch as 1st ch and joining to 1st p of last ch of 3rd row. Do not cut off thread but turn for next row with ch of 8ds, p, 8ds, p, 4ds, join to p of last ch of previous row.

5th ROW
1st Chain. 4ds, 3ps sep by 3ds, 4ds, join by shuttle thread to centre p of next ch of previous row.

Repeat to the end and work to match 1st end.

Cut threads, tie and oversew neatly.

EDGING
1st ROW
1st Ring. *4ds, 3ps sep by 3ds, 4ds, cl. RW.

1st Chain. 4ds, p, 4ds, join to centre p of 1st ch of previous row, 4ds, p, 4ds. RW.

2nd Ring. 4ds, p, 4ds, 6 long ps over card, sep by 1ds, 4ds, p, 4ds, cl. RW.

2nd Chain. 4ds, p, 4ds, join to centre p of next ch on previous row. 4ds, p, 4ds. RW.

Repeat from * to end, finishing with 1st r, turn at end with ch.

2nd ROW
4ds, p, 4ds, join to 2nd p of turning ch of previous row, 8ds, p, 8ds, p, 3ds, join by shuttle thread to centre p of last r of previous row* (3ds, p, 3ds, join to next long p) 6 times, 3ds, p, 3ds, join to centre p of next small r. Repeat from * to end and finishing turning ch to match.

3rd ROW
1st Ring. 4ds, join to top p of turning ch of previous row, 4ds, join to p of next ch, 4ds, cl. RW.

1st Chain. *3ds, join to p of next ch, (3ds, p, 3ds, join to p of next ch) 4 times, 3ds.

2nd Ring. 4ds, join to p of next ch, 4ds, join to p of next ch, 4ds, cl. RW.

Repeat from * to end.

Cut threads, tie and oversew neatly.

A White Collar to enhance a Winter Dress

Materials: Coats Mercer-Crochet No. 20 or 40. 1 ball white. Tatting shuttle.

1st ROW
Fill shuttle with cotton but do not cut it off from the ball.
1st Ring. 4ds, 3ps sep by 4ds, 4ds, cl. RW.
1st Chain. 6ds, p, 6ds. RW.
2nd Ring. 4ds, join to last p of previous r, 4ds, p, 4ds, p, 4ds, cl. RW.
2nd Chain. 6ds, p, 6ds. RW.
Repeat the last r and ch until the required length, finishing with a r, do not reverse work, make a turning

ch of 6ds, p, 3ds, p, 3ds, p, 6ds, join to p of last ch of previous row.

2nd ROW
1st Chain. 6ds, p, 6ds, join to next p of previous row, repeat to the end of the row. Make turning ch to match 1st end and join to base of 1st r.

3rd ROW
Shuttle thread only.
1st Ring. 8ds, join to p of ch before turning ch of previous row, 8ds, cl. RW.
Leave $\frac{1}{4}''$ length of thread between all rs.

2nd Ring. 8ds, p, 8ds, cl. RW.
3rd Ring. 8ds, join to p of same ch of previous row, 8ds, cl. RW.
4th Ring. 8ds, p, 8ds, cl. RW.
5th Ring. 8ds, join to next p of ch of previous row, 8ds, cl. RW.
Repeat the last two rs to the end of the row, and finishing with two rs into the p of the last ch before the turning ch of the previous row. Cut thread and overcast neatly along the side of the last r.

4th ROW

Join threads between the last ch of the 2nd row and the turning ch and work an edge ch of 6ds, 3ps sep by 3ds, 3ds, join to base of 1st r of previous row, 3ds, 3ps sep by 3ds, 3ds, join to p of 2nd r of previous row, 3ds, 4ps sep by 3ds. RW.
1st Ring. 4ds, p, 4ds, join to p of 2nd r of previous row, 4ds, p, 4ds, cl. RW.
1st Chain. 4ds, 3ps sep by 4ds, 4ds. RW.

2nd Ring. 4ds, p, 4ds, join to p of next r of previous row, 4ds, p, 4ds, cl. RW.
2nd Chain. As 1st ch.
Repeat to the end, joining last r to the p of the last r of previous row. RW. Work edge ch to match 1st edge.

5th ROW

1st Ring. 4ds, p, 4ds, join to 3rd p of last edge ch, 4ds, p, 4ds, cl. RW.
1st Chain. 4ds, p, 4ds. RW.
2nd Ring. *4ds, join to last p of previous row, 4ds, p, 4ds, p, 4ds, cl. RW.
2nd Chain. As 1st ch.
3rd Ring. 4ds, join to last p of previous r, 4ds, join to centre p of next ch of previous row, 4ds, p, 4ds, cl. RW.
Repeat from * to end, joining the last r to the 2nd p of the edge ch. Cut threads, tie and overcast neatly. Pin out to shape and press with a damp cloth and warm iron.

Collar in blue and green

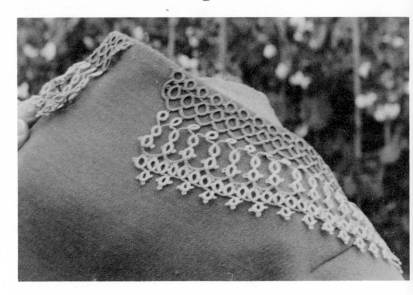

Materials: Coats Mercer-Crochet No. 40. 1 ball blue 594. 1 ball pale green 623. Tatting shuttle.

1st ROW

With blue cotton in shuttle only.

1st Ring. *5ds, 3ps sep by 5ds, 5ds, cl. RW. Leave ⅛″ length of thread.

2nd Ring. 6ds, 3ps sep by 6ds, 6ds, cl. RW. Leave ⅛″ thread.

3rd Ring. 5ds, join to adjacent p of 1st r, 5ds, p, 5ds, p, 5ds, cl. RW. Leave ⅛″ thread.

4th Ring. 6ds, join to adjacent p of 2nd r, 6ds, p, 6ds, p, 6ds, cl. RW. Repeat from * for length required. Cut thread and oversew neatly.

2nd ROW

With blue cotton in shuttle and ball join threads to base of 1st r, and weave in ends.

1st Chain. 6ds, p, 6ds, join by shuttle thread to centre p of 2nd r of previous row.

2nd Chain. 6ds, p, 6ds, join by shuttle thread to centre p of next r on previous row. Repeat this ch to the end, working end ch to match 1st end. Cut threads, tie and oversew neatly.

3rd ROW

With green cotton in shuttle only.

1st Ring. 8ds, join to p of 2nd ch of previous row, 8ds, cl. RW. Leave ¼″ of thread.

2nd Ring. 8ds, p, 8ds, cl. RW. Leave ¼″ of thread.

3rd Ring. 8ds, join to centre p of next ch of previous row, 8ds, cl. RW. Leave ¼″ thread.

Repeat these rs to the end. Cut thread and oversew neatly.

4th ROW

With green cotton in shuttle and blue in ball.

1st Ring. 4ds, p, 4ds, join to p of 2nd r of previous row, 4ds, p, 4ds, cl. RW.

1st Chain. 4ds, 3ps sep by 4ds, 4ds. RW.

Repeat this r and ch to the end. Cut threads, tie and oversew neatly.

5th ROW

With green cotton in shuttle only.

1st Ring. 4ds, p, 4ds, join to 1st p of 1st ch of previous row, 4ds, p, 4ds, cl. RW.

Leave $\frac{1}{8}''$ length of thread between all rings.

2nd Ring. *4ds, 3ps sep by 4ds, 4ds, cl. RW.

3rd Ring. 4ds join to adjacent p of 1st r, 4ds, join to 3rd p of 1st ch of previous row, 4ds, p, 4ds, cl. Do not RW. Leave $\frac{1}{8}''$ of thread.

4th Ring. 4ds, join to adjacent p of previous r, 4ds, join to 1st p of 2nd ch of previous row, 4ds, p, 4ds, cl. RW. Repeat from * to the end, finishing after a 3rd r. Cut thread and oversew neatly.

Press with damp cloth and warm iron. Sew to dress by ps of rs of 1st row, and again by ps of ch of 2nd row.

Lampshade edging No. 1

Materials: Coats Mercer-Crochet No. 20. 1 ball of any shade. The one in the photograph is ecru 610 and the lampshade is crimson pleated nylon. Tatting shuttle.

Many of the edgings in this book would look equally well as edgings for lampshades.
Fill the shuttle with cotton but do not cut it off from the ball.
1st Ring. *8ds, p, 4ds, p, 4ds, cl.
2nd Ring. Close beside 1st, 4ds, join to last p of previous r, 2ds, 8ps sep by 2ds, 4ds, cl.

3rd Ring. Close beside 2nd r, 4ds, join to last p of previous r, 4ds, p, 8ds, cl. RW.
1st Chain. 8ds, p, 8ds, join by shuttle thread to p of previous r.
2nd Chain. 8ds, p, 8ds, RW.
4th Ring. 8ds, join to p of previous r, 4ds, p, 4ds, cl. RW.
3rd Chain. 8ds, p, 8ds, RW.
Repeat from * joining 1st r, after the 8ds, to the base of the previous r. Continue all round, joining the base of the last r to the p of the 1st r, and the last ch to the base of the 3-r cluster.

Lampshade edging No. 2

Materials: Coats Mercer-Crochet No. 40. 1 ball of any shade. The one in the photograph is in white on a pink pleated chiffon shade. ½″ piece of card. Tatting shuttle.

Edging for base of lampshade.
Fill the shuttle with the cotton but do not cut it off from the ball.
1st Ring. 3ds, 3ps sep by 3ds, 3ds, cl. RW.

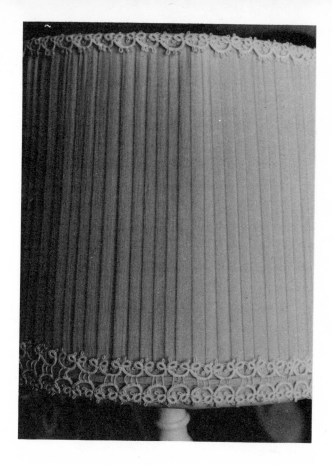

1st Chain. *6ds, long picot worked over card, 3ds, 1p, 3ds, 1p, 6ds. RW.
2nd Ring. 3ds, p, 3ds, join to centre p of previous r, 3ds, p, 3ds, cl.
3rd Ring. 3ds, 3ps sep by 3ds, 3ds, cl. RW.
Repeat from * finishing after 3rd r, join to base of 1st r, join last ch to base of 1st r.

Work second row of edging and join to each of the long ps.
A piece of rolled chiffon or narrow ribbon can be threaded through the long picots before the edging is stitched to the lampshade.
Work a similar edging for the top of the lampshade, but normal length picots instead of the long ones.

Lampshade with Tatted Panels

Materials: Coats Mercer-Crochet No. 20. 1 ball orange 538, but any other clour may be used. 1 lampshade, the one in the photograph is very pale green. Tatting shuttle.

Fill shuttle with the cotton, but do not cut off from ball.

1st Ring. *3ds, 7ps sep by 3ds, 3ds, cl. RW.

1st Chain. 2ds, 6ps sep by 2ds, 2ds. RW.

2nd Ring. 3ds, p, 3ds, join to corresponding p of 1st r, 3ds, 5ps sep by 3ds, 3ds, cl. RW.

2nd Chain. 10ds. RW.

Repeat from * until required length for lampshade, ending with 2nd r. RW.

To turn:

1st Chain. 2ds, 6ps sep by 2ds, 2ds. RW.

1st Ring. 3ds, p, 3ds, join to 6th p of previous r, 3ds, p, 3ds, cl. RW.

2nd Chain. 2ds, 5ps sep by 2ds, 2ds. RW.

2nd Ring. 3ds, p, 3ds, p, 3ds, join to 5th p of previous 2nd r, 3ds, 4ps sep by 3ds, 3ds, cl. RW.

3rd Chain. As previous ch. RW.

3rd Ring. 3ds, 3ps sep by 3ds 3ds, cl. RW.

4th Chain. 2ds, 6ps sep by 2ds, 2ds. RW.

4th Ring. 3ds, p, 3ds, join to centre p of previous r, 3ds, join to 5th p of 2nd last r, 3ds, join to corresponding p of r on opposite side, 3ds, 3ps sep by 3ds, 3ds, cl. RW.

5th Chain. 2ds, 6ps sep by 2ds, 2ds. RW.

5th Ring. 3ds, p, 3ds, join to corresponding p of previous r, 3ds, p, 3ds, join to corresponding p of r on opposite side, 3ds, join to next p of same r, 3ds, 2ps sep by 3ds, 3ds, cl. RW.

6th Chain. 10ds, RW.

Repeat to end.

Make a connecting ch of 2ds, 12ps sep by 2ds, 2ds.

Cut threads, tie to base of 1st r, and overcast neatly.

Press with damp cloth and warm iron, and lightly stitch to the lampshade.

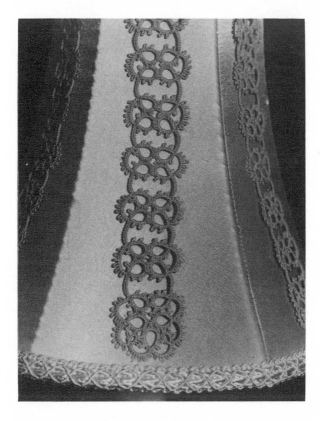

Borders for Towels or Chair Backs

VANDYKE BORDER

Materials: Coats Mercer-Crochet No. 20. 1 ball orange or any other colour may be used. Tatting shuttle. Guest towel. Depth of edging 1¾".

Fill shuttle with cotton and do not cut off from ball.

1st Ring. 4ds, p, 4ds, p, 2ds, p, 4ds, p, 4ds, cl. RW.
1st Chain. 3ds, 6ps sep by 3ds, 3ds. RW.
2nd Ring. 4ds, p, 4ds, join to 3rd p of 1st r, 2ds, p, 4ds, p, 4ds, cl. RW.
2nd Chain. 3ds, p, 3ds. RW.
3rd Ring. As 1st r.
3rd Chain. As 2nd ch.
4th Ring. As 1st r.
4th Chain. 3ds, p, 3ds, join to 5th p of 1st ch, 3ds, 4ps sep by 3ds, 3ds. RW.
5th Ring. 4ds, p, 4ds, join to 3rd p of previous r, 2ds, p, 4ds, p, 4ds, cl. RW.
5th Chain. As 1st ch.
6th Ring. As 5th r.
6th Chain. As 1st ch.

7th Ring. 4ds, p, 4ds, join to 3rd p of previous r, 2ds, join to 2nd p of 4th r, 4ds, p, 4ds, cl. RW.
7th Chain. As 2nd ch.
8th Ring. 4ds, p, 4ds, join to 3rd p of 3rd r, 2ds, p, 4ds, p, 4ds, cl. RW.
8th Chain. As 2nd ch.
9th Ring. As 1st r.
9th Chain. 3ds, p, 3ds, join to 5th p of 6th ch, 3ds, 4ps sep by 3ds, 3ds. RW.
10th Ring. 4ds, p, 4ds, join to 3rd p of 9th r, 2ds, p, 4ds, p, 4ds, cl. RW.
10th Chain. As 2nd ch.
Repeat from beginning five times more then to 10th r once.
11th Chain. As 1st ch.
11th Ring. 4ds, p, 4ds, join to 3rd p of 10th r, 2ds, p, 4ds, p, 4ds, cl. RW.
12th Chain. 3ds, p, 3ds, p, 3ds, RW.
12th Ring. 4ds, p, 4ds, join to 3rd p of 11th r, 2ds, join to 2nd p of 9th r, 4ds, p, 4ds, cl. RW.
13th Chain. As 2nd ch.
13th Ring. 4ds, p, 4ds, join to 3rd

p of 8th r, 2ds, p, 4ds, p, 4ds, cl. RW.
14th Chain. As 12th ch.

14th Ring. 4ds, p, 4ds, join to 3rd p of previous r, 2ds, join to 2nd p of 3rd r, 4ds, p, 4ds, cl. RW.

15th Chain. As 2nd ch.

15th Ring. 4ds, p, 4ds, join to 3rd p of 2nd r, 2ds, p, 4ds, p, 4ds, cl. RW.

16th Chain. As 12th ch.

16th Ring. 4ds, p, 4ds, join to 3rd p of previous r, 2ds, join to 2nd p of 1st r, 4ds, p, 4ds, cl. RW. Repeat from ch 11 to r 16, six times.

17th Chain. As 1st ch.
Cut threads, tie to base of 1st r and overcast neatly.

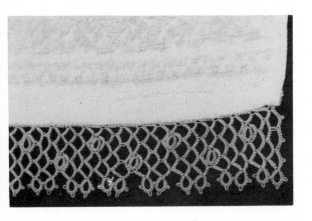

STRAIGHT BORDER

Materials: Coats Mercer-Crochet No. 20. 1 ball blue 459. Tatting shuttle. Guest towel.

Depth of edging 1½".
Fill shuttle with cotton and do not cut off from ball.
Tie a single knot in the cotton, make a small picot, and commence chain.

1st Chain. 4ds. RW.

1st Ring. 7ds, p, 7ds, cl. RW.

2nd Chain. 4ds, p, 4ds, join to p of r.

3rd Chain. 4ds, p, 8ds. RW.

2nd Ring. 4ds, p, 4ds, p, 4ds, p, 4ds, cl. DO NOT REVERSE.

4th Chain. 4ds, p, 4ds, join by shuttle thread to p of previous ch.

5th Chain. 4ds, p, 4ds, join by shuttle thread to p of next ch.

6th Chain. 4ds, p, 4ds, join by shuttle thread to starting p of 1st ch.
Turn work for start of next row.

1st Chain. 4ds, p, 4ds, join by shuttle thread to 1st p of previous row.

2nd Chain. As 1st ch, joining to next p of previous row.

3rd Chain. As previous ch.

4th Chain. 4ds. RW.

1st Ring. 4ds, join to adjacent p of previous r, 4ds, p, 4ds, p, 4ds, cl. DO NOT REVERSE.

5th Chain. 4ds, p, 4ds, join by shuttle thread to p of 3rd ch.

6th Chain. As previous ch, joining to next p.

91

7th Chain. As previous ch, joining to first p of previous row.
Turn work for start of next row.
1st Chain. As previous 1st ch.
2nd Chain. As before. RW.
1st Ring. 7ds, join to p of next ch, 7ds, cl. RW.
3rd Chain. 4ds, p, 4ds, join to same p as previous r.
4th Chain. 4ds. RW.
2nd Ring. 4ds, p, 4ds, p, 4ds, p, 4ds, cl. DO NOT REVERSE.
5th Chain. As before.
6th Chain. As before.

7th Chain. As before.
Turn work for start of next row.
1st chain. As previous 1st ch.
2nd Chain. As before.
3rd Chain. As before.
4th Chain. 4ds. RW.
1st Ring. 4ds, join to last p of previous r, 4ds, p, 4ds, p, 4ds, cl. DO NOT REVERSE.
5th Chain. As before.
6th Chain. As before.
7th Chain. As before.
Continue in this manner for length required.

Handbag with Tatted Cover

Material: Coats Mercer-Crochet No. 20. 1 ball cerise 439, but any other colour may be used. Tatting shuttle.

The pattern for the medallions on this bag are the same as for the Glass Mats, but only work 8ps on the centre ring, and work as far as the 4th round, when you will have 6ds between the small ps.

5th Round. 4ds, p, 4ds, between all small ps.

Make 12 medallions for each side of the bag. Join together by the 2chs each side of the 3rd r of edging and leave 3 rs between joinings.

Materials for bag:
½ yard strong linen type material.
¾ yd buckram.
½ yd lining.
1 handbag frame 9″.

To make the bag:

Cut a piece of buckram 22″ × 9½″ and cover on one side with a thin layer of cotton wool, stitch round the edges to hold secure.

Cut a piece of linen approximately 3″ longer than the buckram, and 1″ wider at each side.

Turn a 1″ hem at each end and make a ⅜″ channel for the handbag rod to go through.

For gusset cut two pieces of linen 11″ × 7″ using 1″ at top for hem and ¾″ all round for turnings.

Put gusset into bag 1″ down from top.

Put buckram into bag and hand stitch into place, using a stab stitch, through buckram making sure that the gusset seam lies about ¼″ over the edge of the front cover.

Make lining to match and hand stitch into place.

Make eyelets in the top channel for the rod to go through and turn down the corner of the bag to fit.

Because of the buckram interlining the bag will not gather on to the rods, so the top must be made to fit by varying the position of the eyelets. Press the tatted medallions with a damp cloth and warm iron and stitch to the outside of the bag.

Summer Handbag

Materials: Coats Mercer-Crochet No. 20. 1 ball dark ecru 626. Tatting shuttle.

First Medallion

The centre of these medallions is worked in a continuous chain.

Fill the shuttle with cotton, but do not cut it off from the ball.

CENTRE RING

2ds, 7ps sep by 2ds, 2ds, the 8th p being made by making a knot in the two ends of thread, and without cutting off the cotton continue into the next round.

1st Round. 3ds, join by shuttle thread to 1st p of starting r, small p, 3ds, join to next p and repeat all round starting r.

Do not cut off thread, but continue into next round.

2nd Round. smp, 4ds, join by shuttle thread to next smp, repeat all round.

3rd Round. smp, 5ds, join by shuttle thread to next smp, repeat all round.

Repeat until 8th round has been worked.

9th Round. 6ds, p, 6ds, join to next smp of previous round.

Repeat all round.

Cut threads, tie and overcast neatly.

EDGING

1st Ring (large). *12ds, p, 4ds, p, 4ds, p, 4ds, cl. RW.

1st Chain. Join ball thread to base of r and weave in ends. 2ds, 5ps sep by 2ds, 2ds. RW.

2nd Ring. 4ds, join to 1st p of large r, 4ds, cl. RW.

2nd Chain. As 1st ch.

3rd Ring. As 2nd r, joining to 2nd p of large r.

3rd Chain. As 1st ch, join to 3rd p of large r.

The blocks of 5 chs are worked as follows, after joining the 3rd ch to the large r, make a p followed by 8ds, turn the work, p, 8ds, join by shuttle thread to the end p, turn the work and repeat until a block of 5 chs are complete. RW.

Chain. 2ds, 3ps sep by 2ds, join to any p on centre medallion, 2ds, 3ps sep by 2ds, 2ds. DO NOT REVERSE.

Work a 2nd block.

p, 8ds, join by shuttle thread to end p of previous block, turn.

p, 8ds, join to p at beginning of block.

Repeat until 5 chs are completed. DO NOT REVERSE.

Repeat from * joining the 1st ch of the next block of chs to the free corner of the previous block.

Repeat all round centre medallion.

Join the motifs together by the 2 centre ps of the 2nd ch. Repeat on following 2nd ch.

Three motifs were used on the handbag in the picture, but more could be used if desired.

Materials for bag:

Cut 1 piece of linen or suitable material approximately 26″ × 12½″.

Cut 2 pieces for gusset 10½″ × 2½″—iron all pieces on to Vilene.

Cut lining same size.

Insert the gusset into the bag allowing 4″ to turn down for the flap.

Place a piece of stiff card 1½″ wide in the base of the bag and stitch into position. Make the lining and stitch into the bag by hand. Pleat the top of the gusset so that the flap will lie flat.

The handle is made of a crochet tube of double crochet with a piece of plastic clothes line pulled through.

The two rings for the handle are metal rings covered with crochet.

Put the handle through the rings and attach a crochet covered button to the ends of the handle.

Stitch a covered button to the front of the bag and make a crochet loop. Press the tatting and stitch to the flap of the bag.

Covered Buttons

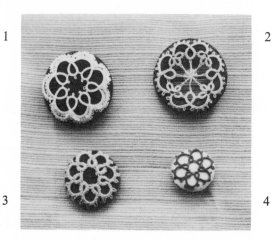

These covered buttons look very attractive as a decoration on a plain dress and almost any small medallion can be used for this purpose.

First cover a button mould with the same material as the dress, or for contrast, cover with velvet, make your tatted medallion and carefully sew to the button.

BUTTON NO. 1

This is covered with navy blue jersey, and the tatting is in white.

Size of button 1½".

Fill the shuttle with white Mercer-Crochet cotton No. 60, but do not

cut it off from the ball.

1st Ring. 10ds, p, 4ds, p, 4ds, p, 10ds, cl. RW.

1st Chain. 3ds, 9ps sep by 2ds, 3ds. RW.

2nd Ring. 10ds, join to last p of previous r, 4ds, p, 4ds, p, 10ds, cl. RW.

2nd Chain. As 1st ch. RW.

Continue until 7rs and 7chs have been made, joining last r to 1st r and last ch to base of 1st ch.

Do not cut off cotton.

2nd Round

1st Chain. 3ds, 11ps sep by 2ds, 3ds,

join by shuttle thread to base of next r. Repeat this ch all round.

Tie ends and leave enough thread to stitch the medallion to the button.

Press with damp cloth and warm iron. Stitch to the button by the ps in the centre and enough of the outer ps to hold the medallion secure.

BUTTON NO. 2

This is made from an old buckle, the outer edge being covered with crochet cotton, also the centre bar.

Materials: Coats Mercer-Crochet No. 20. 1 ball brown 579 for the cover of the buckle. 1 ball turquoise 521 in No. 40 for the medallion.

Wind a small amount of cotton on to the shuttle, but do not cut the thread off from the ball.

1st Ring. *5ds, 3ps sep by 5ds, 5ds, cl. RW.

1st Chain. 3ds, 5ps sep by 3ds, 3ds. RW.

2nd Ring. 6ds, join to last p of previous r, 6ds, cl.

3rd Ring. Close beside 1st, 6ds, p, 6ds, cl.

4th Ring. As previous r. RW.

2nd Chain. As first ch. RW.

Repeat from * 3 times more, joining the centre p of the last r, to the first p of the first r, and the last ch to the base of the first r. Cut the threads leaving them long enough to stitch the medallion to the button.

Centre

Thread a needle with a length of the crochet cotton.

Pick up the ps in the centre of the medallion, and crossing from side to side, make the frame on which to work the cobweb stitch. Securely fasten the threads in the centre, and with the head of the needle, work back over one bar and under two, for about six rounds. Fasten off on the back.

Press with a damp cloth and warm iron. Stitch to the buckle.

BUTTON NO. 3

This is covered with brown velvet and the tatting is in beige pure silk, but any of Coats Mercer-Crochet cotton in No. 20 would be suitable. Put a small amount of the silk on to the shuttle and leave enough silk to make the chains—approximately $1\frac{1}{2}$ yards. Size of button $1\frac{1}{4}''$.

1st Ring. 4ds, p, 2ds, p 4ds cl. RW.

1st Chain. 3ds, 3ps sep by 3ds, 3ds, RW.

2nd Ring. 4ds, join to last p of previous r, 2ds, p, 4ds, cl. RW.

2nd Chain. As 1st ch.

Repeat until 7rs are worked, joining last p of last r to first p of first r, and joining last ch to base of first r.

Tie threads and leave enough thread to stitch medallion to button.

Press very lightly and stitch to button by the outer row of ps.

BUTTON NO. 4

This button is covered with peach coloured satin and the tatting is worked with brown Sylko.

Size of button 1″.

Wind a small amount of Sylko on to the shuttle, but do not cut the thread off from the reel.

1st Ring. 6ds, p, 4ds, p, 6ds, cl. RW.

1st Chain. 6ds, 3ps sep by 6ds, 6ds. RW.

2nd Ring. 6ds, join to last p of previous r, 4ds, p, 6ds, cl. RW.

Repeat until 6 rs have been worked, joining the last p of the last r to the 1st p of the 1st r, and the last ch to the base of the 1st r. Leave ends long enough to stitch the medallion to the button.

Press lightly and stitch to the button by the outer ps only.

Finger Plate for door

Materials: Coats Mercer-Crochet No. 40. 1 ball turquoise 521. 2 tatting shuttles.

Length 9½″, width 2½″.

CENTRE ROW

Fill shuttle with cotton but do not cut off from ball.

1st Ring. 8ds, p, 8ds, cl. RW.

1st Chain. 4ds, p, 4ds, long p, 4ds, p, 4ds. RW.

2nd Ring. *8ds join to p of previous r, 8ds, cl.

3rd Ring. Close beside 2nd r, 8ds p, 8ds, cl. RW.

2nd Chain. As 1st ch.

Repeat from * until there are 32rs. RW.

End Chain. *4ds, p, 4ds, long p, repeat from * twice more, 4ds, p, 4ds. RW.

Work 2nd side to match, joining rs to make groups of 4. Work 2nd end ch to match 1st. Cut threads, tie to base of 1st r and overcast neatly.

2nd ROW

With shuttle thread only.

1st Ring. 4ds, join to long p of 1st ch of centre row, 4ds, cl. RW.

Leave ¼″ thread between all rs.

2nd Ring. 5ds, p, 5ds. RW.

Repeat these two rs all around centre row, but working two rs into centre long p of turning ch on centre row. Cut thread and still leaving ¼″ thread fasten to base of 1st r and oversew neatly.

OUTER ROW

With 2 shuttles.

Join threads to p of 1st free r on previous row, and weave in ends.

1st Chain. With first shuttle, 4ds.

*With second shuttle make a josephine knot of 12 first half knots.

With first shuttle, 4ds.

Repeat from * twice more.

Join by shuttle thread to p of next free r on previous row.

Repeat all along side. To turn at the

ends work 4 josephine knots on the end 4 chs.

Cut threads, join to where 1st ch was joined, tie, and overcast neatly. Pin out to shape and press with damp cloth and warm iron.

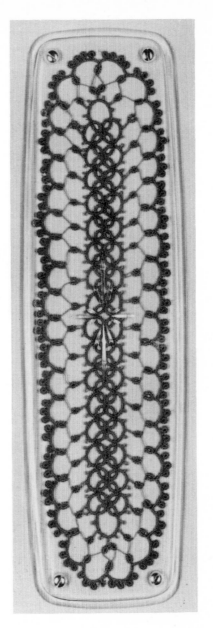

Drip Mats

Materials: Coats Mercer-Crochet No. 40. 1 ball selected colour. Tatting shuttle. Small piece of linen.

Fill shuttle with cotton, but do not cut it off from the ball.
Commence with the flower motif on the outside row.

1st Ring. 3ds, 3ps sep by 4ds, 3ds, cl. RW.
1st Chain. 5ds, p, 5ds, p, 5ds. RW.
2nd Ring. *3ds, p, 4ds, join to centre p of 1st r, 4ds, p, 3ds, cl. RW.
2nd Chain. 5ds, p, 5ds, p, 5ds. RW. Repeat from * twice more, join by shuttle thread to base of 1st r. This completes a flower.
5th Chain. 9ds, p, 3ds. RW.
5th Ring. 9ds, p, 5ds, p, 4ds, cl. RW.
6th Ring. 3ds, join to p in preceding ch, 6ds, p, 3ds, p, 6ds, cl. RW.
6th Chain. 10ds. RW.

7th Ring. 12 ds, p, 12ds, cl. RW.
7th Chain. 10ds. RW.
8th Ring. 6ds, p, 3ds, p, 6ds, p, 3ds, cl. RW.
9th Ring. 4ds, join to last p of 5th r, 5ds, p, 9ds, cl. RW.
8th Chain. 3ds, join to last p of 8th r, 9ds. DO NOT REVERSE.
10th Ring. 3ds, 3ps sep by 4ds, 3ds, cl. RW.
9th Chain. 5ds, p, 5ds, join to corresponding p of last ch of previous flower motif, 5ds. RW.
Complete flower as before. Join to base of first ring of flower. Cut threads, tie and overcast neatly.
Make two more groups but with 1r uppermost and to the right of preceding group join the first p of 4th ch of flower motif, the 2ps of 6th r, and the p of 1r to corresponding ps.

These three groups make a half circle. Make another half circle in this manner.

Make the linen base by cutting a piece of linen, 3″ in diameter and putting a small hem all round, or, 2½″ in diameter and buttonhole stitch around.

Glass Mats

Materials: Coats Mercer-Crochet No. 20. 1 ball of any colour. A set in six different colours looks very attractive. Tatting shuttle.

The centre of these mats is worked in a continuous chain.

Fill the shuttle with cotton, but do not cut it off from the ball.

CENTRE RING

2ds, 8ps sep by 2ds, 2ds, make the 9th p by tying the two ends of the cotton together, and without cutting off the threads continue into the next round.

1st Round. 3ds, join by shuttle thread to 1st p of starting r, small p, 3ds, join to next p and repeat all round starting r. Do not cut off thread, continue into next round.

2nd Round. Small p, 4ds, join by shuttle thread to next small p, all round.

3rd Round. As previous round, with 5ds between all small ps.

Repeat until 8th round has been worked.

9th Round. 6ds, p, 6ds, join to small p of previous round.

Repeat all round.

Cut threads, tie and overcast neatly.

EDGING

1st Ring. *6ds, p, 6ds, cl. RW.

1st Chain. Join ball thread to base of r and weave in both ends, 2ds, 6ps sep by 2ds, 2ds, join to p of previous r.

2nd Ring. 3ds, join to any p of centre, 3ds, cl; join by shuttle thread to same p as previous ch.

2nd Chain. 2ds, 6ps sep by 2ds, 2ds, join by shuttle thread to base of first r. RW.

3rd Chain. 4ds, 5ps sep by 2ds, 4ds. RW.

3rd Ring. 3ds, join to 3rd p of 2nd ch, 3ds, p, 3ds, p, 3ds, cl. RW.

4th Chain. As 3rd ch.

Repeat from * joining 3rd p of 1st ch to last p of 3rd r, and joining last p of last r to 3rd p of 1st ch and last ch to base of first r.

Cut threads, tie and overcast neatly. Press with damp cloth and warm iron.

Lady's Choker

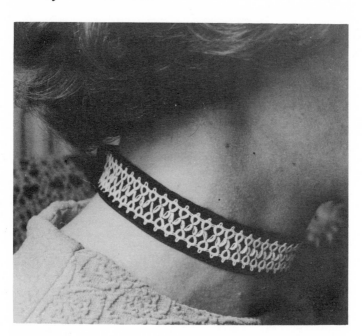

Materials: Coats Mercer-Crochet No. 40. 1 ball white. 1 tatting shuttle. Length of black velvet.

This edging is worked with shuttle thread only.

1st Ring. 5ds, p, 2ds, p, 2ds, p, 5ds, cl. RW.

Half Ring. 6ds, pull ring up half way. DO NOT REVERSE.

2nd Ring. As 1st r. RW.

Half Ring. As 1st half r.

3rd Ring. *5ds, join to adjacent p of 1st r, 2ds, p, 2ds, p, 5ds, cl. RW.
Half Ring. As 1st half r.

Repeat from * for length required.
Stitch to velvet, sew on small hook and worked loop to fasten.

Framed Medallion

Materials: Coats Mercer-Crochet No. 20. This medallion is worked in shade No. 621 (blue) but any other shade may be used. 2 tatting shuttles. Piece of card ⅜″ wide.

WITH SHUTTLE AND BALL
1st Round. 1 ds, 6ps sep by 2ds, 1ds, cl. Cut ends, tie, and overcast neatly.
2nd Round. Draw about 2 yds of cotton from shuttle and pass this thread through any p of previous round. Use this length of cotton in place of ball thread.
*2ds, 1 long p (worked over ⅜″ card, as described in instructions, page 17). 2ds, 1 long p, 2ds, attach by shuttle

thread to next p of 1st round.
Repeat from * 5 times more.
Fasten to base of 1st ch of round.
Cut ends, tie, and overcast neatly.

WORK WITH 1 SHUTTLE
3rd Round
1st Ring. *3ds, join to any long p of previous round, 3ds, cl. RW.
2nd Ring. Leave ¼″ length of thread, 4ds, p, 4ds, cl. RW.
Again leave ¼″ length of thread and repeat from * 11 times.
Cut thread, and still leaving ¼″ of thread, join to base of 1st r.

103

WORK WITH 2 SHUTTLES
4th Round. Join to any p of previous round.
1st Chain. *3ds, p, 3ds.
1st Ring. With 2nd shuttle.
3ds, join to p of ch, 3ds, p, 3ds, p, 3ds, cl.
2nd Ring. Work close to 1st r. 3ds, join to adjacent p of 1st r, 3ds, p, 3ds, cl.
3rd Ring. Work close to second r, 3ds, join to adjacent p of 2nd r, 3ds p 3ds, p, 3ds, cl.

WORK WITH 1st SHUTTLE
2nd Chain. 3ds, join to last p of 3rd r, 3ds. Join with shuttle thread to p of next r of previous round.
Repeat from * working all round, joining 2nd p of 1st r to 2nd p of 3rd r of previous 3-r group, and 2nd p of last r to 2nd p of 1st r and last ch to same p as 1st ch.

WORK WITH BALL AND SHUTTLE
5th Round. Join thread to a p between two motifs.
1st Chain. 2ds, p, 2ds, p, 2ds, join to p between 1st and 2nd rs.
2nd Chain. 2ds, 4ps sep by 2ds, 2ds, join to p between 2nd and 3rd rs.
3rd Chain. 2ds, p, 2ds, p, 2ds, join to p between motifs.
Repeat from *.
Join last ch to base of 1st ch.
Cut threads, tie, and overcast neatly.

Recommended Books

TATTING by Elgiva Nicholls—out of print.
THE ART OF TATTING by Lady Hoare—out of print but still to be found in reference libraries.
A NEW LOOK IN TATTING by Elgiva Nicholls.
TATTING by Irene Waller.
COATS SEWING GROUP BOOKS.
THE ENCYCLOPEDIA OF NEEDLEWORK by Therese D. Dillmont.

Suppliers in the UK and USA

The Needlewoman, 21 Needless Alley, Birmingham.
Denley & Son Ltd., 24 Priory Ringway, Birmingham.
The John Lewis Partnership, Oxford Street, London, W.1. and all their branches.
Aluminium shuttles—Abel Morrall Ltd., Clive Works, Redditch, Worcs.
F. J. Fawcelt Inc., 129 South Street, Boston, Mass. 02111.
  —or your local department store or craft shop.